SHIBUSA / HIVE ARCHITECTS

TH ECONOMY OF FORM

MASTERPIECE
SERIES

SHIBUSA / HIVE ARCHITECTS
INTRODUCTION BY **ROBERT McCARTER**
COMPLETED BUILDING PHOTOGRAPHY BY **RYAN GAMMA** AND **HIVE ARCHITECTS**

OSCAR RIERA OJEDA
PUBLISHERS

CONTENTS

INTRODUCTION	010
BY ROBERT McCARTER	
DESIGN	016
DESCRIPTION	018
SKETCHES	020
PRESENTATION DRAWINGS	022
RENDERINGS	032
CONSTRUCTION	046
WORKING DRAWINGS	048
PROCESS	076
THE BUILDING	122
APPENDIX	218
BIOGRAPHY	220
PROJECT CREDITS	222
PHOTOGRAPHY CAPTIONS	224
BOOK CREDITS	240

INTRODUCTION
BY ROBERT McCARTER

Dwelling On The Horizon Line
As exemplified in the works of Joe Kelly and Gwen Leroy-Kelly of Hive Architects, based in Sarasota, the constructively critical practice of modern architecture continues to be uniquely capable of making places where contemporary cultural, social, and domestic aspirations are realized in harmony with the climate, topography, and environment of Florida. Since modern architecture first emerged in Florida as a fusion of modern concepts with vernacular principles, the works of practitioners such as Hive Architects have exemplified modern architecture's characteristics of appropriate engagement of the climate and environment of its place; revelatory expression of structure and construction, and respect for the nature of materials; capacity to house new, differing and changing rituals of daily life across generations; individual spatial freedom combined with a collective sense of being rooted in place; and reinforcement of our identity as those who, as the Florida architect Donald Singer said, "live in the modern age."[1] The work of the best of recent generations of Florida practitioners, such as Hive Architects, is inspired by the regionally inflected modern architecture that emerged at the mid-20th-century in the regions around Miami, Fort Lauderdale, Jacksonville, Tampa, and especially the Sarasota School comprised of Paul Rudolph, Gene Leedy, Mark Hampton, Victor Lundy and Carl Abbott, among others, while also being grounded in the particularities of their place and the circumstances of their time.

The Kellys, whose careers began after 2000, start from an optimistic and engaged position with respect to the tradition of modern architecture that they have inherited from their predecessors such as the Sarasota School. The Kellys' work epitomizes the fusion of continuity and innovation that lies at the heart of the modern tradition, as realized through their spirited and constructive rediscovery, redeployment, and redefinition of modern architecture. Yet this same modern architecture is seen by too many other architects today as only another "style" for superficial application, and here one is reminded of the Austrian philosopher—and sometime architect—Ludwig Wittgenstein's statement: "Today the difference between a good and a poor architect is that the poor architect succumbs to every temptation and the good architect resists it."[2] The reduction of modern architecture to a set of stylistic forms for endless and meaningless recombination by Wittgenstein's poor architects—typical of far too many buildings in Florida—is the exact opposite of the way in which the principles of modern architecture are put into practice by Wittgenstein's good architects, among whom the Kellys should be placed. In their work, Hive Architects may be said to engage both the timeless modern tradition, embodied in exemplary built works such as those of the Sarasota School, and the unique circumstances of our time, as determined by the clients' characteristic way of living, the site, climate and environment, the program, the codes, the budget, the imperatives of sustainability, and the appropriate materials and methods of construction in each case.

ROBERT McCARTER is a practicing architect, author, and, since 2007, Ruth and Norman Moore Professor of Architecture at Washington University in St. Louis; he has previously taught at the University of Florida (1991-2007), where he was also the founding Director of the School of Architecture; Columbia University (1986-1991) where he was also Assistant Dean; and as visiting professor at University of Arkansas Fay Jones School of Architecture; the IUAV (Venice); the Berlage Institute (Rotterdam); University of Louisville; and North Carolina State University, as well as being Visiting Scholar at the American Academy in Rome on three occasions. Since 1982 he has had his own architectural practice in New York, Florida and St. Louis, with 25 realized buildings. He is the author of twenty-three books, including *Place Matters: The Architecture of WG Clark* (2019); *Grafton Architects* (2018); *Marcel Breuer* (2016); *The Space Within: Interior Experience as the Origin of Architecture* (2016); *Steven Holl* (2015); *Aldo van Eyck* (2015); *Alvar Aalto* (2014); *Carlo Scarpa* (2013); *Understanding Architecture: A Primer on Architecture as Experience* (2012, with Juhani Pallasmaa); *Louis I. Kahn* (2005), and *Frank Lloyd Wright* (1997). McCarter was one of 71 International Exhibitors for the 2018 Venice Biennale of Architecture, and he was named one of the "Ten Best Architecture Teachers in the US" by *Architect* magazine in December 2009.

In arriving to their present constructively critical manner of practicing architecture, the Kellys benefitted from being educated at the University of Florida, which during their time there was one of the relatively rare schools of architecture that maintained a balanced relationship between theory and practice (understanding that theory comes from practice, and not the other way around), between the academy and the profession (understanding that they are related in a reciprocal and complementary manner, as two sides of a coin), and which as a result was a leader in the renewed engagement of practice by schools that took place in the late 1990s—precisely when the Kellys entered architecture school. The Kellys' architectural education was shaped by the school's engaging disciplinary principles through case studies from history; continuing evolution of the modern movement as a critical practice of the "unfinished project" (Habermas); developing appropriate ways of engaging the exceedingly subtle, ecologically fragile, water-saturated, and virtually flat landform that constitutes the environment of Florida, primarily through rejecting imported styles and embracing common sense principles drawn from the vernacular; taking on the myriad challenges facing contemporary practice; applying constructive criticism to both student and professional work; exploring the possibilities of innovative and traditional craft and construction techniques; and inviting the best practicing professionals to participate in both the teaching of studios and the criticism of student projects.

Unique to the University of Florida during this time was the legacy of spatial teaching of Bernard Voichysonk, student of Josef Albers at Yale and professor of architecture at the school for 45 years, who developed Albers' fundamental spatial insight, "The plane, the in-between of volume and line, traverses the separation of two and three dimensions," through the deployment of the folded plane. The teaching of Voichysonk and his faculty colleagues realized Albers' intention to have the students explore the use of simple, austere, fundamental elements—lines and planes—folded and projected in countless ways, as if to prove the ability to generate space is inexhaustible. Elements in the student designs were often deceptively simple, in and of themselves, yet they were ordered, projected, and folded in increasingly complex relationships, resulting in precise shapes that offered multiple readings and in spatial forms that could not be comprehensively perceived from only one viewpoint. The result of this teaching was an eye for the total inhabited space—the discovery that it is the relationship among the enclosing planes and spatial forms that is more important than the formal purity of the individual elements. The folded plane intentionally crosses between walls, ceilings, floors, and the spaces they enclose and imply, and the resulting constructions can only be appropriately deciphered in the occupation and experience of inhabitation. The consistent emphasis of the teaching was on the spatial experience of the interior—as planes folding and unfolding to shape inhabited space—from within which the inhabitant looks out to the infinitely extended horizon line of the Florida landscape.

In all these ways, the school may be said to have engaged in a constructive critique of normative modes and patterns of design process and professional practice from within by encouraging the graduates of the program to practice architecture in such a way as to change and transform the profession by example—by built example, the only kind that matters in architecture. As a result of their constructive architectural education, and their ensuing positive transition to professional practice, the Kellys begin with the belief that modern architecture is a shared discipline to be practiced, and that architecture should be directed towards making the world a better place.

The way in which the Kellys have put the principles of modern architecture into practice by grounding them in a particular place, re-engaging them with the timeless ethical imperatives of appropriateness, and transforming them through their process of design evolution involving the collective efforts of the clients, the construction and crafts team members, and the architects, can be revealed by an examination of the subject of the present book, the recently completed Shibusa House. Built to the designs of Hive Architects on a narrow waterfront site at the northern tip of Siesta Key, the house opens onto Big Sarasota Pass that connects Sarasota Bay and the Gulf of Mexico.

The first impression of Shibusa, as seen from the stone-paved entry court to the south, is of the domestic volumes being enclosed in a thick, sharp-edged white folded plane comprising the floor, wall and ceiling and opening to the west and south. This domestic volume is elevated a full floor above the ground and cantilevered out towards the south while simultaneously extending deep into the interior of the site to the north. Standing at ground level, the interior of the site is shielded from eye-level view by a continuous line of vertically striated aluminum screen-walls that run the width of the site and beneath the cantilevered volume of the house, where it merges with the garage doors. In this way the concept of the house as a series of domestic spaces elevated above the ground, hovering on the horizon line, and opening to the Pass to the north and the bayou to the south, is clearly presented in the very first view, yet without resulting in any loss of privacy for the inhabitants within.

The means by which the thick folded planes of the house are elevated above the thin slats of the aluminum screen-walls is revealed when we enter through the gate adjacent to the garage. A continuous structural and shear wall of rough-patterned horizontal board-formed concrete surrounds the garage, supports the concrete floor slab above, and divides the enclosed portion of the ground floor on the right from the outdoor terrace, entry passage and swimming pool to the left. From this vantage point at the entry, the outdoor pool terrace—in experience closer to a courtyard—extends from south to north beneath the elevated volume that runs across the site from west to east, the concrete walls and hovering floor slab together framing the view of Big Sarasota Pass that opens at the end. The primary elevated volume, containing the living spaces of owner's suite, living room, dining room and kitchen extends across the narrow width of the site, and the secondary elevated volume, containing the entry hall, media room and guest suites, extends along the length of the eastern side of the site. The organization of the house is at once clear and straightforward, responding to the requirement to place all the living spaces a full floor above the ground to mediate the effects of storm surge, and to the clients' desires for clearly separated primary and secondary living spaces, accommodated in the two wings of the L-shaped floor plan, which in turn wraps around and frames the exterior terrace-pool-court.

The elongated lap pool begins at the wood-floored sun deck adjacent to the entry and sculpture courts at the south end of the terrace-courtyard, extends along the length of eastern concrete wall, past the wood-slat-screened entry hall, passing into the shadows beneath the primary living spaces, alongside the board-formed concrete pier that carries the living volumes above, and finally out to terminate beyond the forward edge of the house at a waterfront deck set on the existing sea wall. The shadow cast by the large hovering volume of the primary spaces above covers one-half of the length of the pool, allowing its use during the most intense mid-day sunlight. Adjacent to the pool, and similarly covered and shaded by the elevated primary volume, is the outdoor living room which opens to the waterfront to the north and is cooled by the ocean breezes. More open than enclosed, being defined more by the trees and narrow gardens along the east and west edges of the site and the waterfront to the north, than by the walls of the house behind, and with its floor the same white and sea-green terrazzo as the upper level floors, this outdoor living room is perhaps the most comfortable and inviting space in the house, and one that can be used year-round in the tropical Florida climate.

In plan, the two wings—the longer and narrower one containing the secondary spaces running north-south, and the shorter and deeper one containing the primary spaces running east-west—are joined at their meeting point by the double-height entry hall and stair, and pinned together by the elevator, the horizontal board-formed concrete walls of which rise from the ground to the roof. Illuminated by full height glazing on both east and west, and suspended over river-washed stones that carry from inside to outside, the treads of the open stair—the first four treads of concrete, cantilevered off the concrete wall, and the landing and upper treads of folded hot rolled steel, cantilevered off the steel tube stringer—form a spatial pivot that, starting at the front door, invites the inhabitants to traverse six 90-degree turns, and six changes of orientation, which sequentially unfold as they enter, ascend, and arrive to the living room, where they are given a carefully framed panoramic view of the Pass to the north.

The primacy of the main living and owner's bedroom spaces that are housed in the wider east-west volume is indicated by it being covered by a higher, thermo ash wood-clad ceiling, surrounded by clerestory windows, which tilts subtly upwards towards the view to the

Pass. The kitchen, dining room, living room and owner's bedroom extend from east to west across the oceanfront of the house, and they are connected by the deep covered terrace, through which the rooms are given framed views of Big Sarasota Pass in the foreground, shorelines and mangrove swamps across the water, and the skyline of downtown Sarasota in the distance—all woven together by the horizon line. Engaging with the circumstances of the site, the Kellys allow those inhabiting Shibusa to have the largest and longest views to the horizon to the north, with the sunlight always from the south, or behind the viewer, and thus brilliantly illuminating the water, passing boats, distant buildings, mangroves, and shorelines without glare.

The elevated wood-clad ceiling of the primary spaces is framed by a lower white ceiling, matching the height of the ceilings in the rest of the house, which runs around the perimeter of the primary spaces and covers the kitchen, owner's bed, and northern terrace. The owner's bedroom is separated from the living and dining rooms by a wall of glass fiber reinforced concrete tiles and gypsum board that stops short of the front glass wall, the rear white oak-paneled wall, and the higher ash wood ceiling to allow the outer surfaces of the larger volume to be continuous. Acoustical privacy is discretely provided by the frameless glass plane above the dividing wall, as well as by the sliding oak wood pocket door. As a result, the primary living and bedroom spaces are experienced as being one large room elevated above the ground, opening to the north, and hovering on the horizon line seen in the distance.

The primacy of this main living and owner's bedroom wing is complemented by the provision of a largely solid-walled volume, clad and cased in white oak panels, set along the south edge of the wing, which contains the bathing, storage, and service elements and which separates the waterfront living spaces from the entry hall and secondary wing behind. In traversing the upper level, the two wings of the house are in turn joined by the large, oak-walled opening into the living room from the stair hall, which is aligned along one edge with the continuous covered terrace that runs along the west side of the secondary wing and overlooks the entry and pool courts, and garden. In counterpoint to this precise distinction between the primary and secondary wings, the entire house is integrated by being built with a carefully coordinated and harmonized palette of finish materials that impart to the house a sense of repose.

This integration begins with the terrazzo floor, white in color and speckled with sea-green aggregate, that runs continuously throughout the elevated interior of the house, tying all the rooms together, while subtly recalling the white beach sand of the Siesta Key site. Apart from the double-height entry hall, where the horizontal board-formed concrete and vertical thermo ash wood rise from the concrete floor below, all the other walls of the house are a combination of white-painted gypsum board, white cabinets, white oak casework and paneling, and full-height glazing set in aluminum frames. The only exception is the long horizontal window above the white quartz kitchen counter, which is designed to allow a seated-eye-level view of the eastern horizon while carefully editing out the neighboring house. The almost invisible railings at the entry stair and its opening, and along the elevated terraces, are large sheets of frameless laminated glass. The narrow vertical wood slat screen-walls clipped onto the outer faces of selected windows, along portions of the outer edges of the terraces on the upper floor, and continuing down to frame the entry below, provide privacy and sun-shading, as well as a visual counterpoint to the horizontal floor and roof slabs and horizontal shadow-lines of the board-formed concrete walls on the ground level.

The white concrete integral sinks and countertops, white cabinetry, and white-upholstered or light wood furnishings, have been carefully selected to complement the subdued colors of the rooms. Aside from the raised thermo ash-clad ceiling at the primary living volume, the ceilings are white-painted gypsum board throughout, matching the cantilevered white stucco soffits of the terraces outside and complementing the continuous white terrazzo floor beneath them. In a particularly subtle detail, the cylindrical steel pipe columns that rise from the concrete floor slab to support the roof are painted aluminum color to match the aluminum glazing mullions. The subdued and light-colored material palette allows a few elements to stand out, including the dark grey hot rolled steel treads of the entry stair, powder room door, and vertical sliding door pulls, all of which were custom fabricated for the house. The refined and harmonious material palette of the interior extends to the exterior, where the horizontal board-formed concrete walls are complemented by the vertical wood slat-screens and thermo ash terrace walls, and the sea-green flecked white terrazzo floor is complemented by the shell-like white stucco surfaces of the folded floors, walls and roof soffits floating overhead.

The experience of Shibusa is one that admirably and comprehensively provides for the "use and comfort" of the inhabitants, which Frank Lloyd Wright said are the essential but too-often overlooked characteristics of a good house. Here use and comfort are combined with the positioning of the inhabitants in the larger landscape necessary for dwelling, by providing simultaneous visual "prospect" without and hidden "refuge" within.[3] Together these comprise what Wright considered to be the primary requirement of good domestic design—the provision of a sense of "shelter" and "repose" for those who dwell in it—which may be said to characterize the experience of Shibusa. Also shared with Wright, as well as with Renaissance palazzos and villas and the early houses of Le Corbusier, is the Kellys' deployment of the concept of the piano nobile or noble floor, where the primary rooms of the house are elevated one level above the ground floor (with its covered outdoor living room in Shibusa), as can be seen in Wright's early Robie House and later Lewis House, as well as Rudolph's Leavengood House and Biggs House. The Kellys have made a house that engages the horizontal line as the sheltering line, paradoxically aligned with the earth while hovering above it, and at one and the same time opening and connecting to the distant horizon line. This is shelter defined by the broadly cantilevered roofs, opening out to the horizon, yet complemented in the case of Shibusa by the enclosure provided by the folded planes. Perhaps the clearest indication of the Kellys' maturity and capacity as architects is their accomplished embrace of what is likely Wright's most difficult charge to architects—that a house should not draw attention to itself, but rather should serve as the "background and framework" for the rituals of daily life that take place in it.

Today it is often suggested that architecture is not worthy of attention and analysis if it does not benefit from a very large budget which allows the unrestrained use of the most advanced technology and the richest, rarest, and non-renewable materials. Beyond being patently unsustainable on every level, such an attitude goes against the long tradition of embracing and engaging limits in modern architecture, exemplified by Wright's statement, "The human race built most nobly when limitations were greatest and, therefore, when most was required of imagination in order to build at all. Limitations seem to have always been the best friends of architecture."[4] This contemporary celebration of excess consumption in architecture also goes against the modern tradition as defined by Louis Kahn when he stated that a good work of architecture is not dependent on the employment of the finest materials or most advanced technology, but rather is the result of the quality of the design conception and construction craft that goes into the making of it.[5] An architecture that is appropriate both for the place in which it is built and the people who inhabit it is one which allows the maximum engagement of the environment, and which constructs the maximum experiential enrichment of daily life, while requiring the minimum economic and energy expenditure, and resulting in minimal impact on the environment.

As practiced by Joe and Gwen Kelly, modern architecture, rather than being a set of universally applicable formal elements to be overlaid on contemporary constructions, or a "style" lodged in a particular moment in history, can best be defined as an architecture appropriate to its time and its place. Modern architecture, in both historical and contemporary examples, such as Shibusa, demonstrates the significant benefits of an evolutionary, rather than revolutionary, development of architecture. This is because, like all living traditions and constructive disciplines, modern architecture cannot survive—much less thrive—without its principles being put into practice by each new generation of architects. As exemplified in the work of Hive Architects, it is only through this kind of constructive engagement of modern architecture's fundamental principles in a particular place and at a certain time by each new generation that it is continually grounded, transformed, and reborn.

Robert McCarter
Ruth and Norman Moore Professor of Architecture
Washington University in St. Louis

---

[1] Donald Singer, quoted in Robert McCarter, "Concrete Places in a Landscape of Illusions," in *The Architecture of Donald Singer, 1964-1999* (Fort Lauderdale: Bienes Center for the Literary Arts, 1999), 28.

[2] Ludwig Wittgenstein (1930), *Culture and Value* (Chicago: University of Chicago Press, 1980), 3e.

[3] Jay Appleton, *The Experience of Landscape* (Chichester: Wiley, 1996).

[4] Frank Lloyd Wright, *The Future of Architecture* (New York: Horizon Press, 1953), 62.

[5] Louis Kahn, quoted in Robert McCarter, *Louis I. Kahn* (London: Phaidon, 2005), 43.

DESIGN

DESCRIPTION

After the purchase of a long and narrow property along Big Sarasota Pass, the Owners' desire was for the design of their future home to reflect their simple, uncomplicated but refined lifestyle. With simplicity of form and materials, the conceptual idea for this project derives from the Japanese word *shibusa*. This concept encompasses an enriched, subdued appearance or experience of intrinsically fine quality with economy of form, line, and effort, producing a timeless and tranquil aesthetic.

With the lift of the structure above base flood elevation as a zoning requirement, the Owners' aspiration was to inhabit modest but carefully interconnected pavilions that levitate above the tropical landscape. The simplicity of form is achieved through the configuration of the L-shaped structure that is composed of two rectilinear pavilions. Containing the public aspects of the program as well as the Owners' quarters, the main pavilion is carefully carved out to open itself toward the water views of Big Sarasota Pass. This uninterrupted view to the horizon becomes the common datum that links the spaces of the open floor plan and the adjacent rooms. Separated from the main pavilion by a transparent two-story entry stair, the private elements of the program are gathered in a long and narrow volume. The orientation of the guest pavilion takes advantage of the internal courtyard containing a tropical garden with lap pool while also providing additional water views. The cantilevered extension of this volume above the private courtyard entry screen enhances the essence of the floating structure as if it was reaching out to capture the views of Bayou Louise on the opposite side of the property.

The delicate expression and detailing of architectural elements further reinforce the simplicity of the structure while addressing the local climate. Strategically placed vertical shading screens, deep overhangs, and nested windows emphasize the integrity of the structure by their adaptation and interplay with the Florida sun. The careful composition of repetitive but limited material palette of exposed board-on-board concrete on the ground floor, vertical composite wood shading screens and wood siding on the elevated structure, and white portland cement plaster provide a gesture of unity as well as an understated elegance and timelessness.

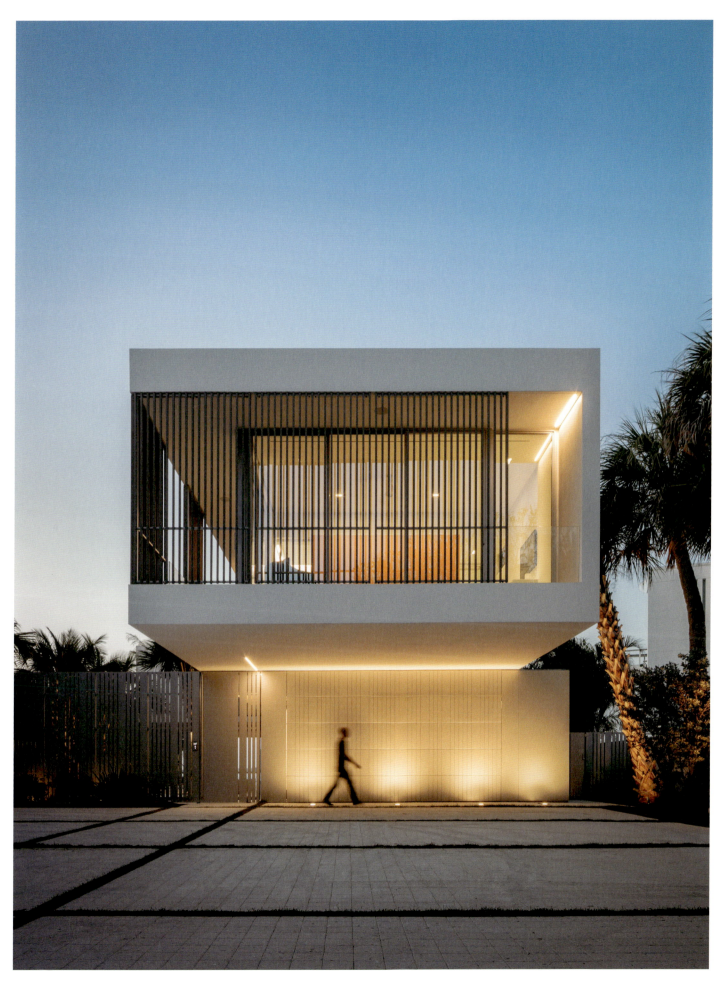

SKETCHES

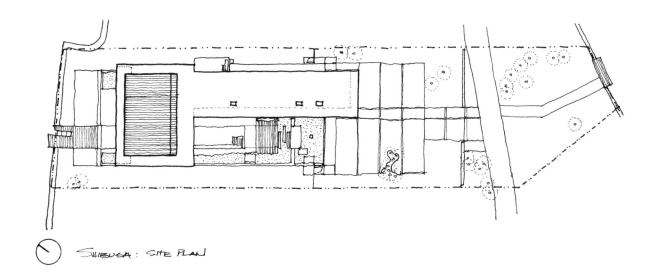

Shibuya: Site Plan

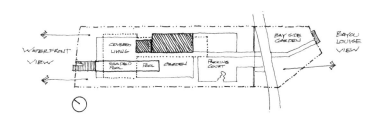 

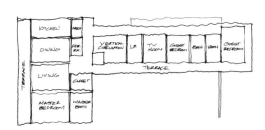 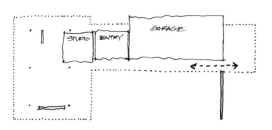

PRESENTATION DRAWINGS

Site Plan

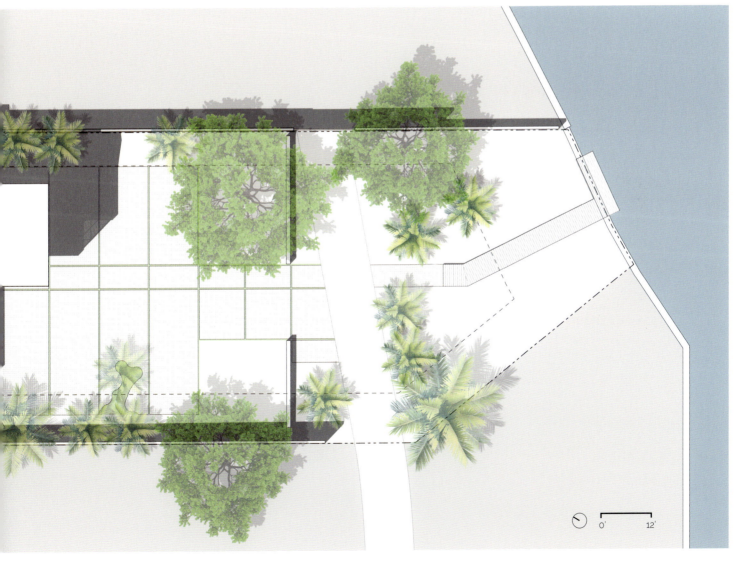

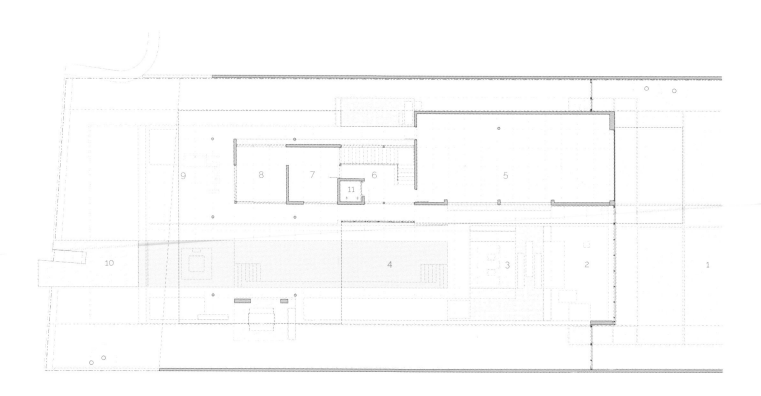

Ground Floor Plan

1. Driveway & Parking Court
2. Entry Sculpture Garden
3. Sun Deck & Entry Courtyard
4. Lap Pool
5. Garage
6. Entry
7. Exercise Room
8. Studio
9. Outdoor Living Room
10. Waterfront Deck
11. Elevator

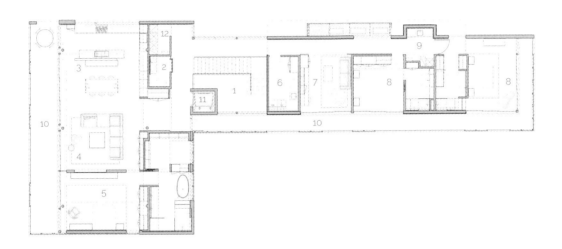

First Floor Plan

1. Entry Stair
2. Powder Bath
3. Kitchen & Dining
4. Living Room
5. Master Bedroom Suite
6. Laundry Room
7. TV Room
8. Guest Bedroom Suite
9. Guest Coffee Bar
10. Exterior Terrace
11. Elevator
12. Mechanical Room

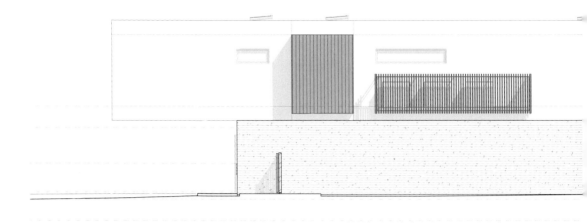

East Elevation

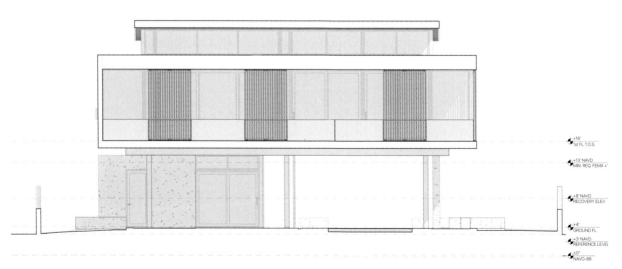

North Elevation

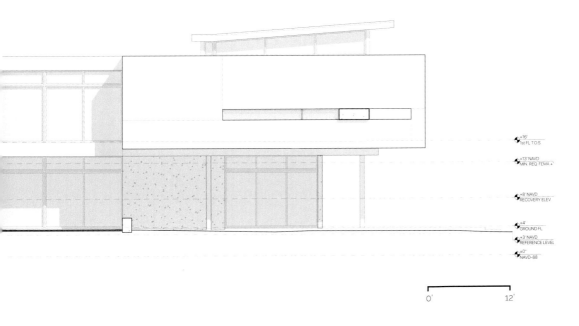

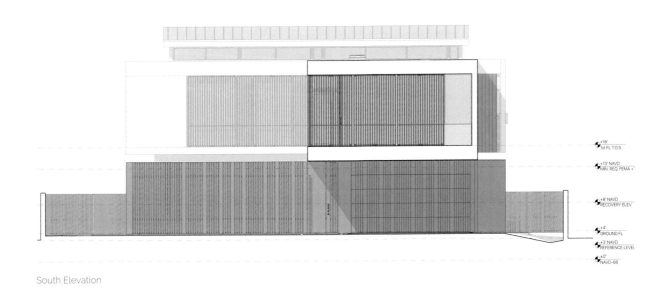

South Elevation

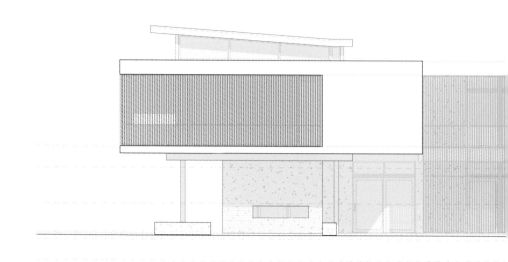

West Elevation

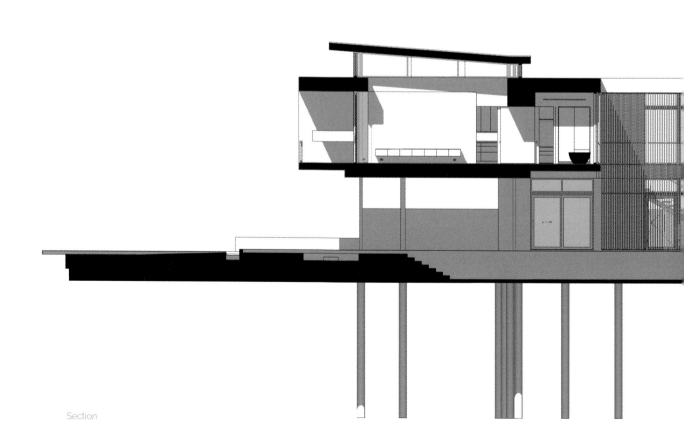

Section

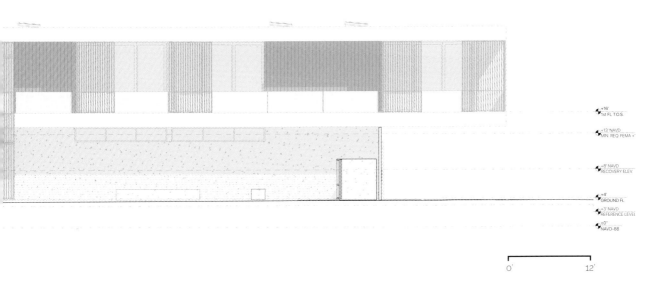#

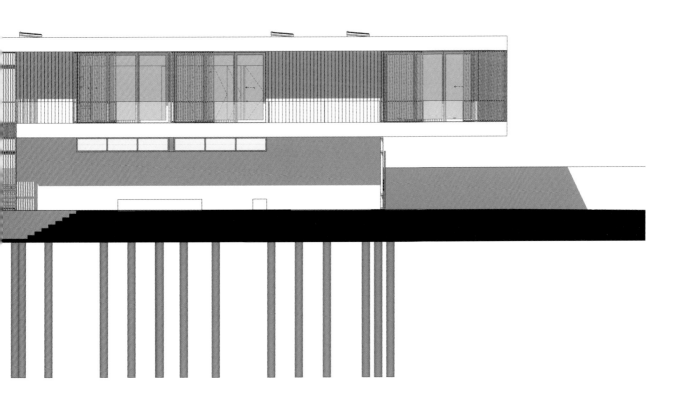

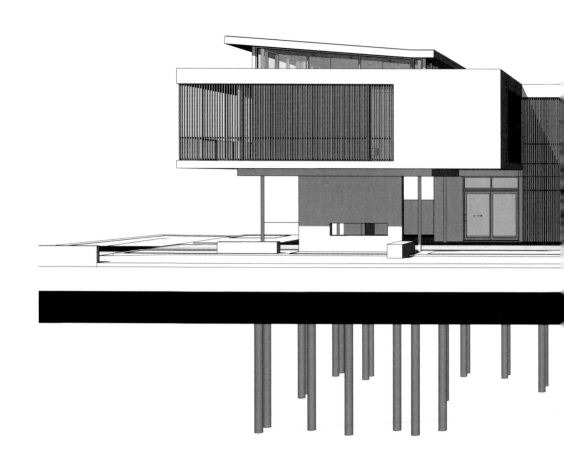

Section

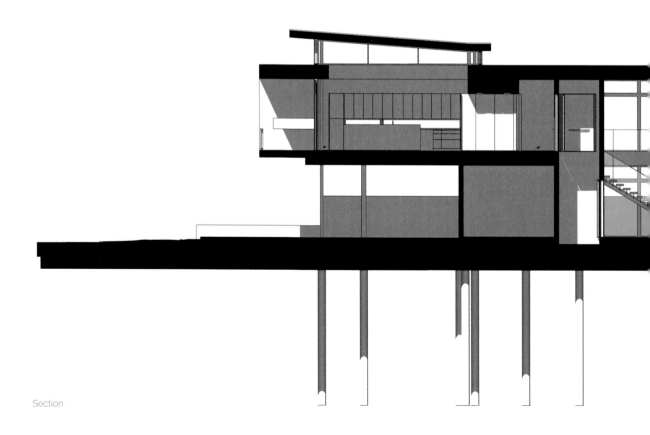

Section

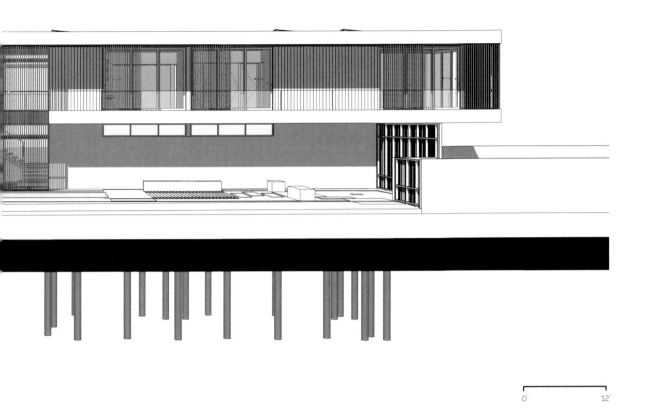

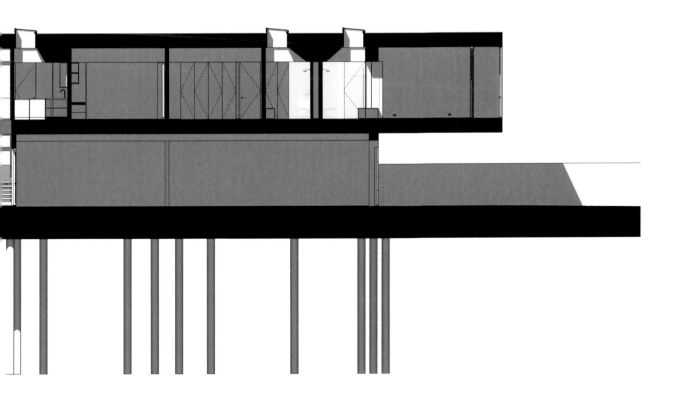

RENDERINGS

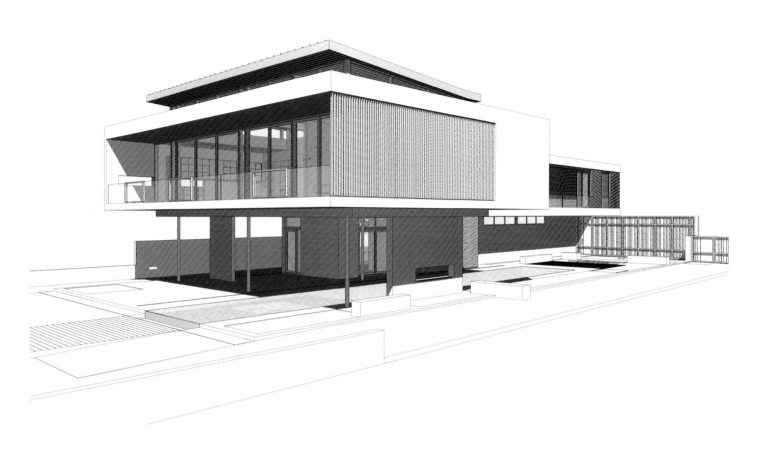
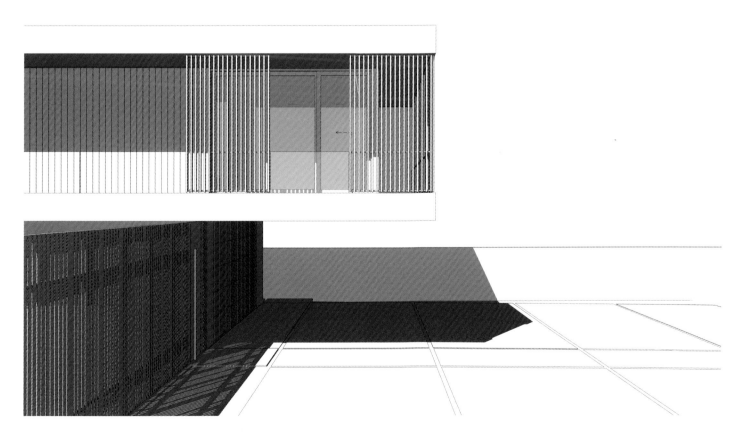

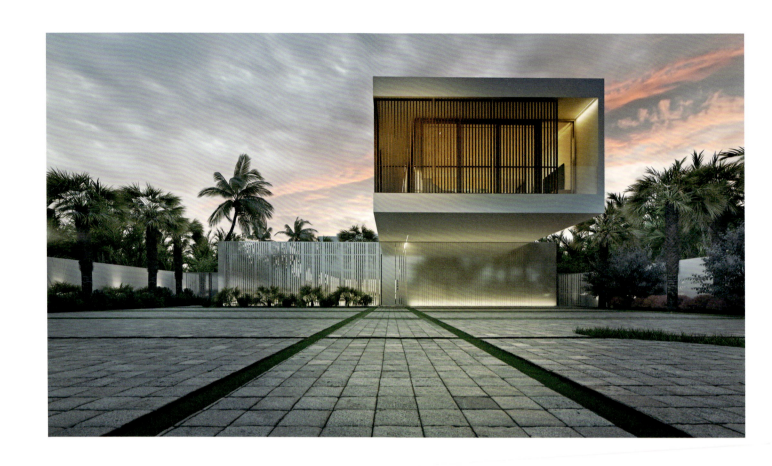

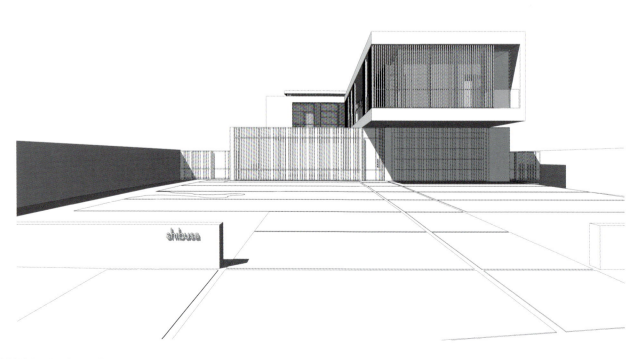

034 | DESIGN / RENDERINGS

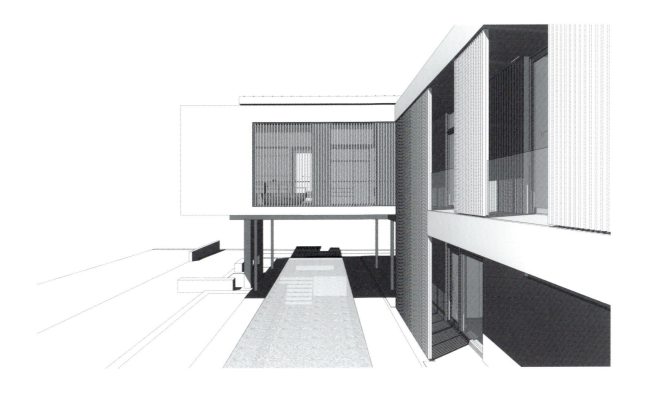

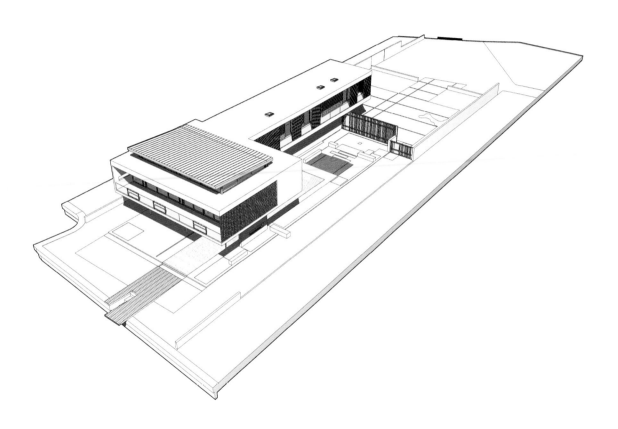

CONSTRUCTION

WORKING DRAWINGS

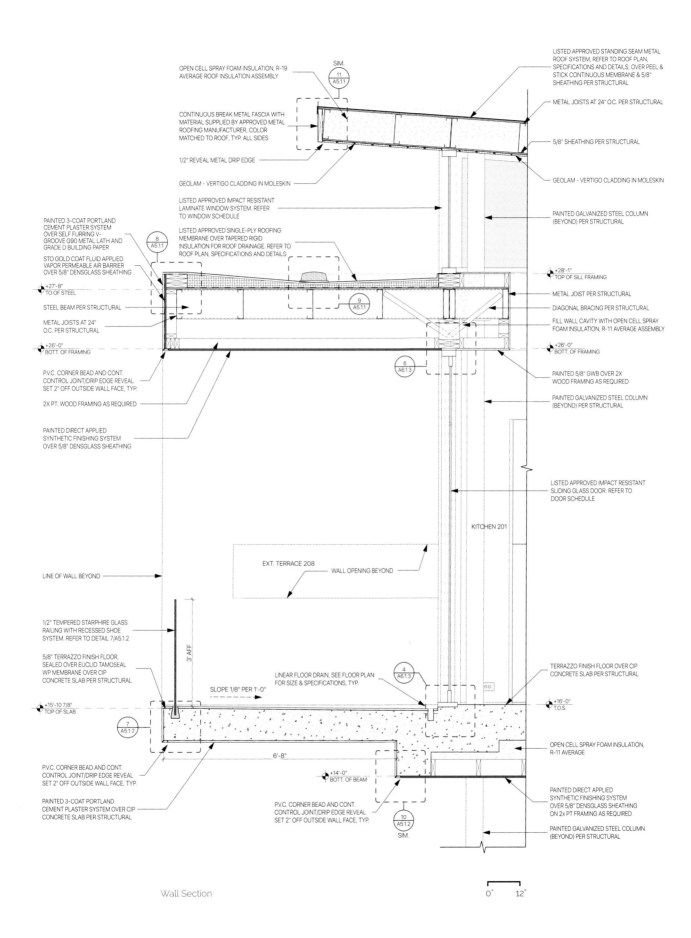

Wall Section

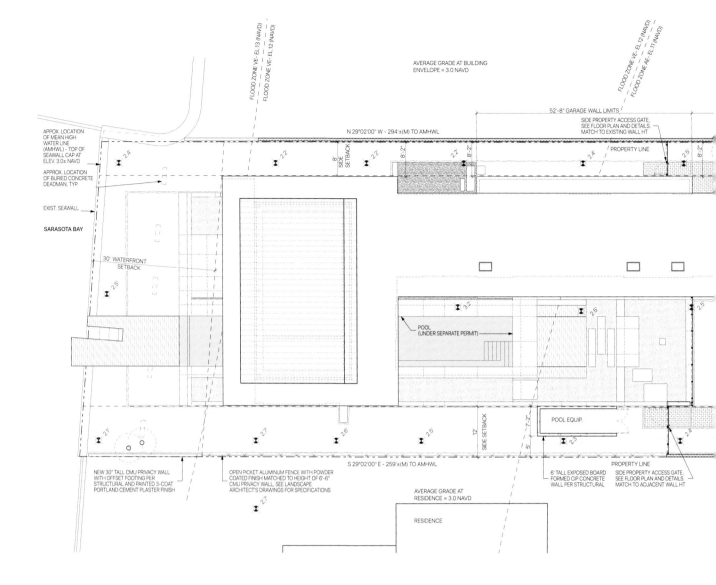

Site Plan

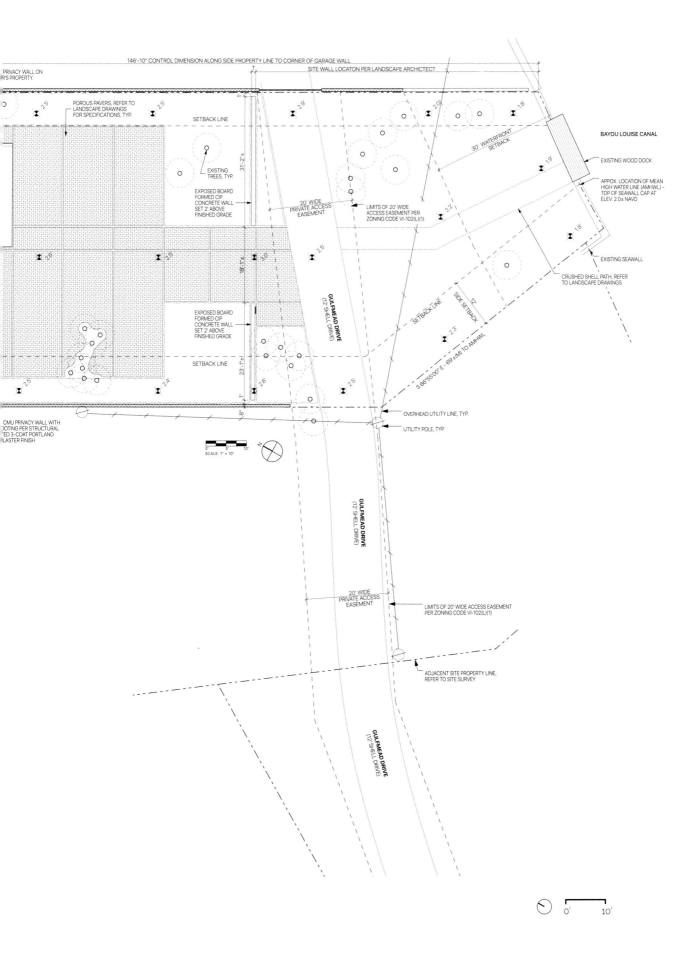

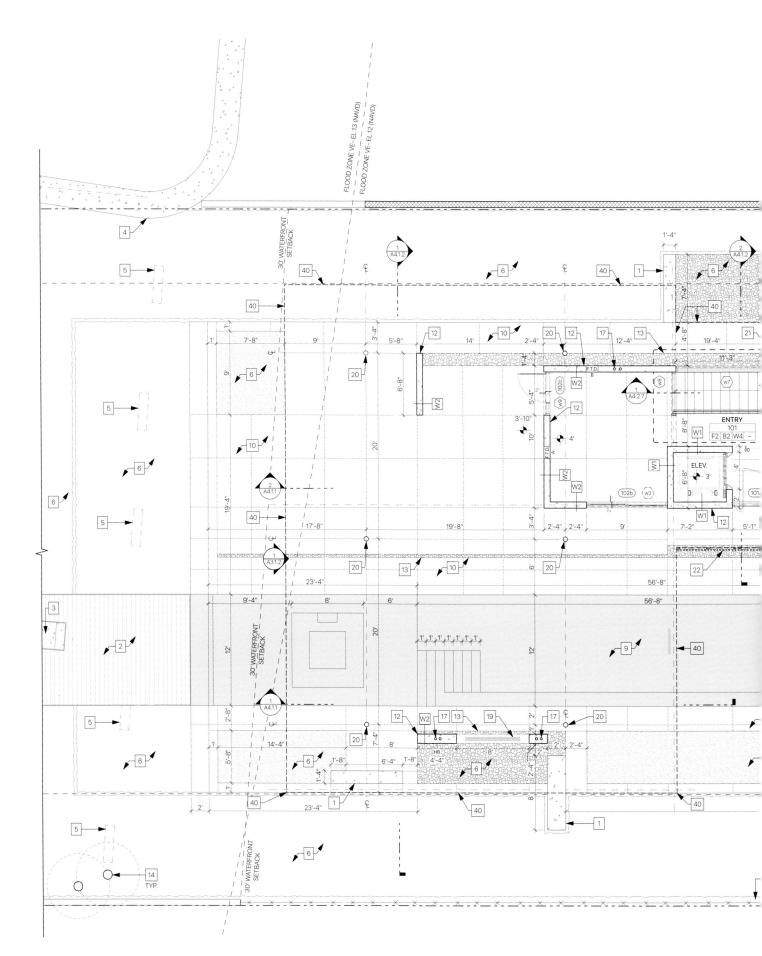

Ground Floor Plan

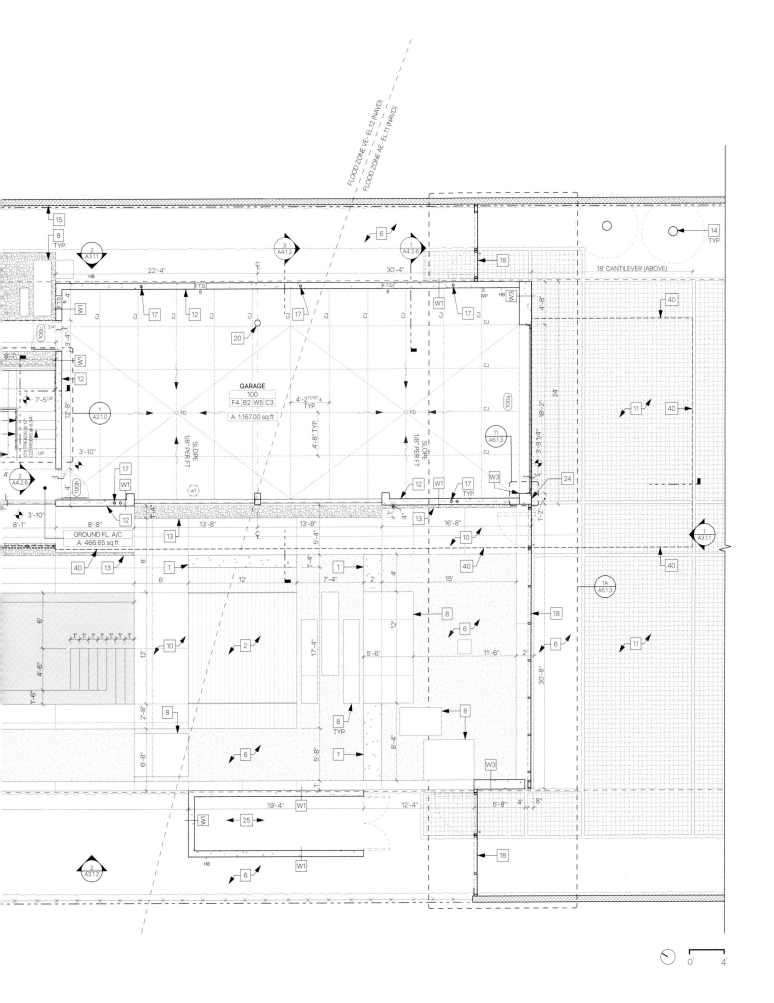

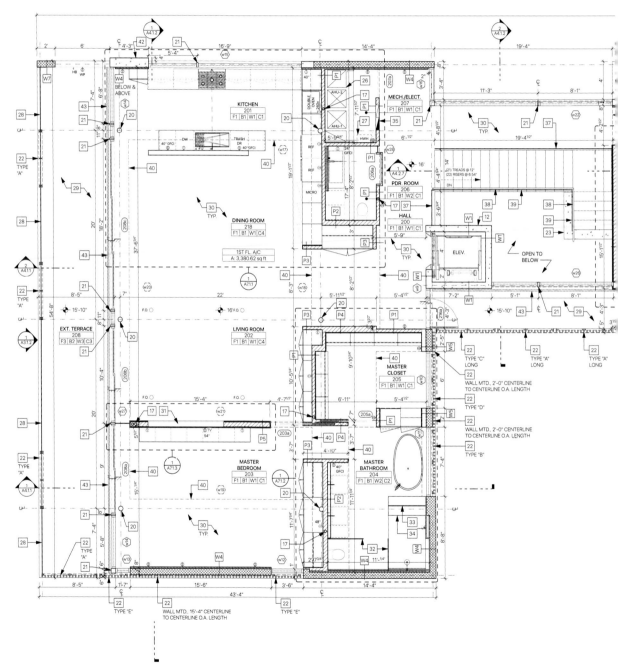

First Floor Plan

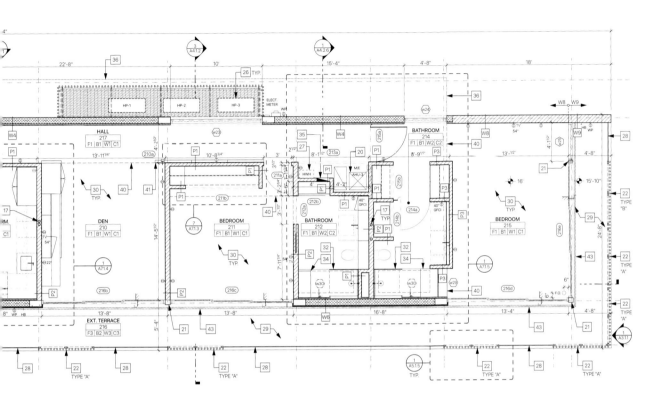

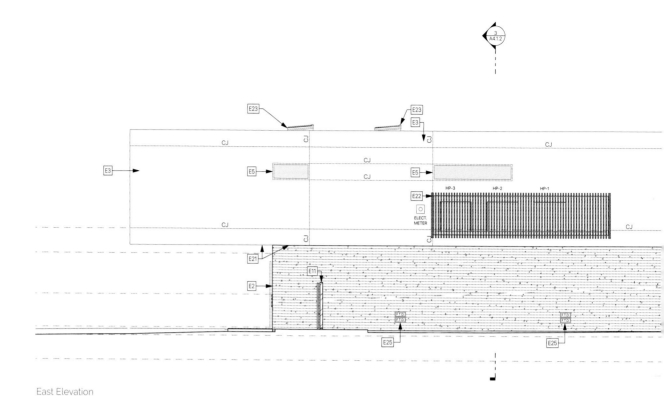

East Elevation

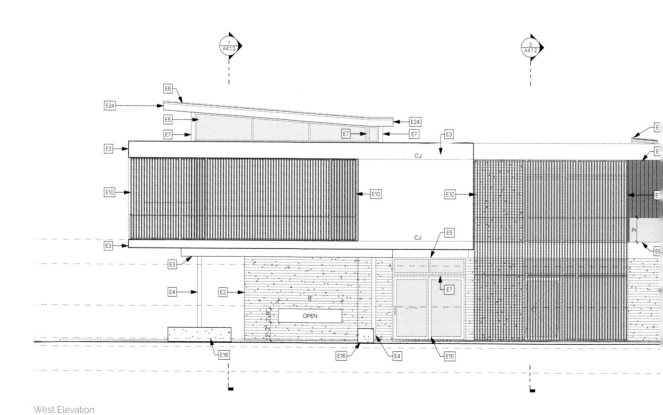

West Elevation

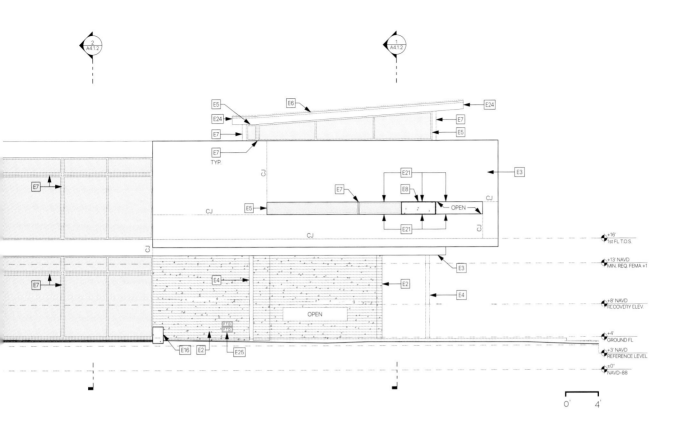
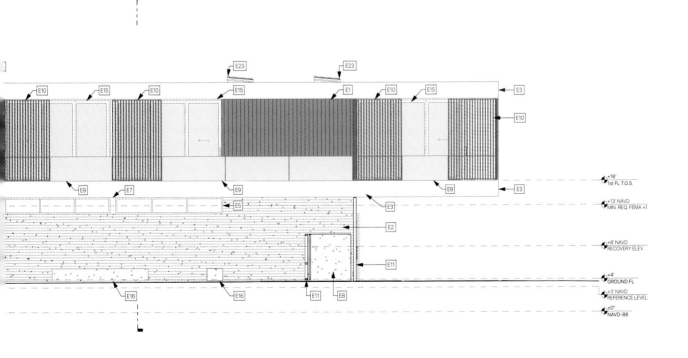

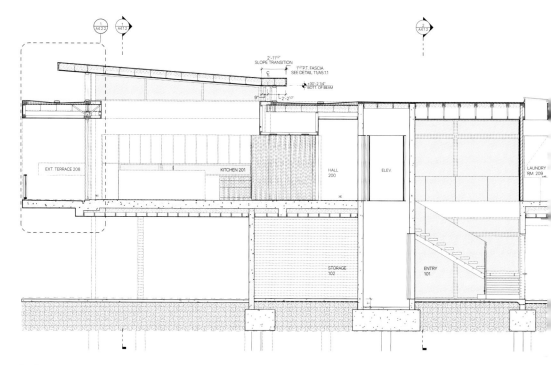

Section

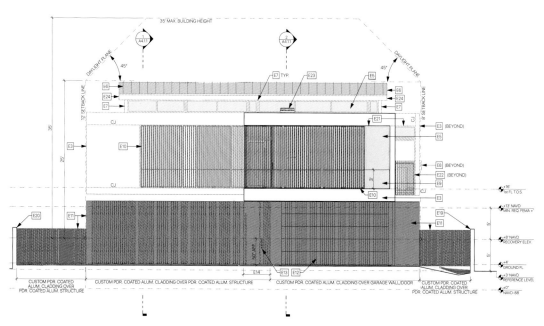

South Elevation

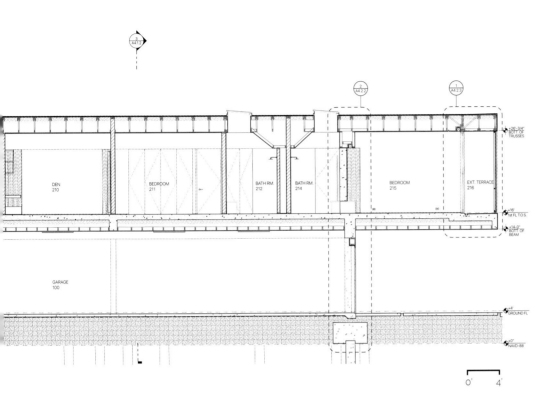

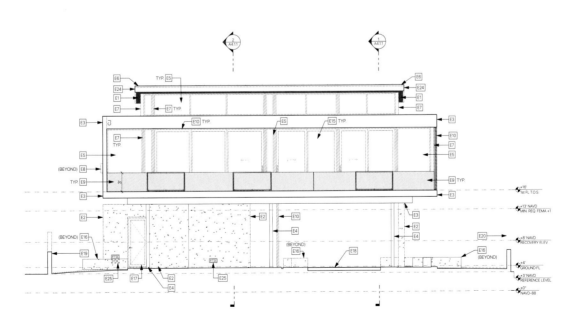

North Elevation

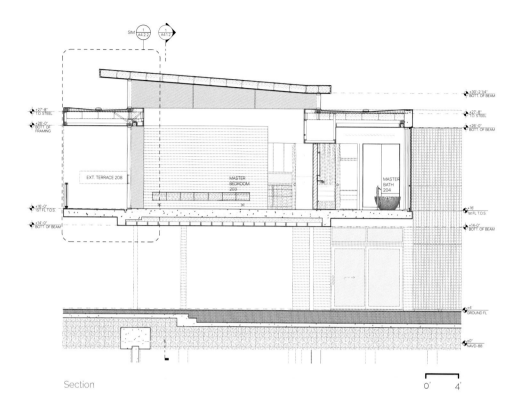

Section

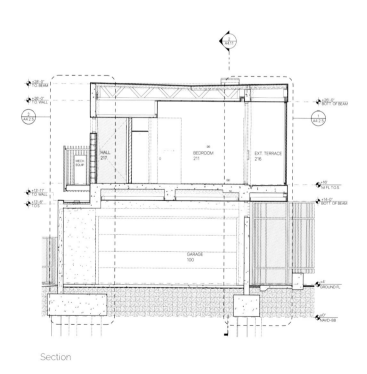

Section

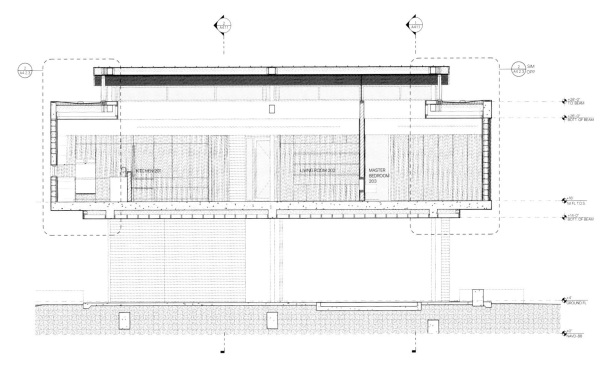
Section

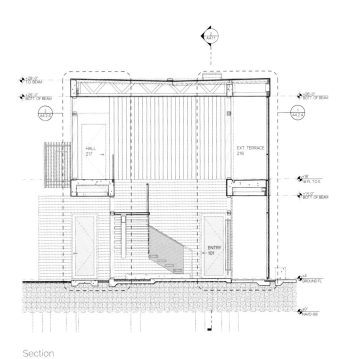
Section

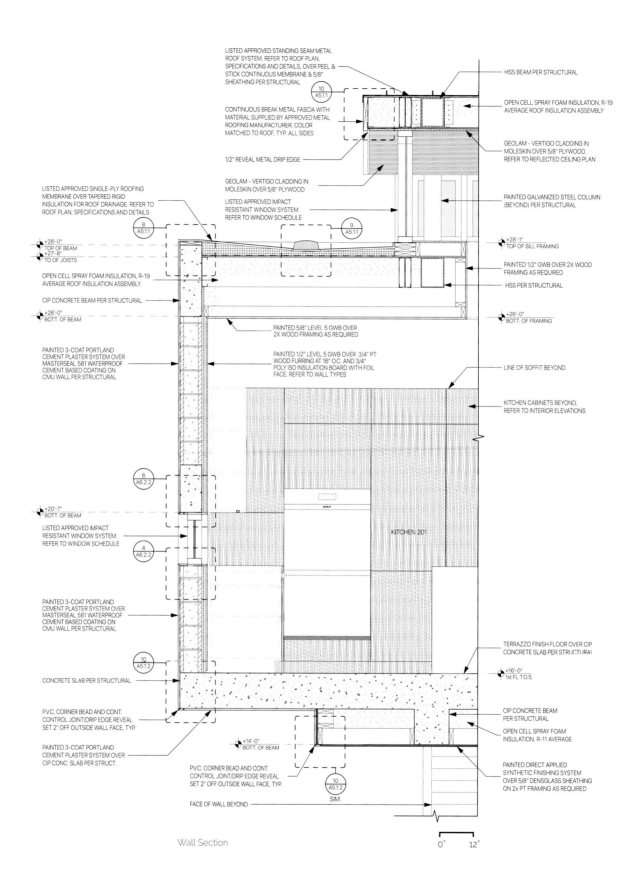

Wall Section

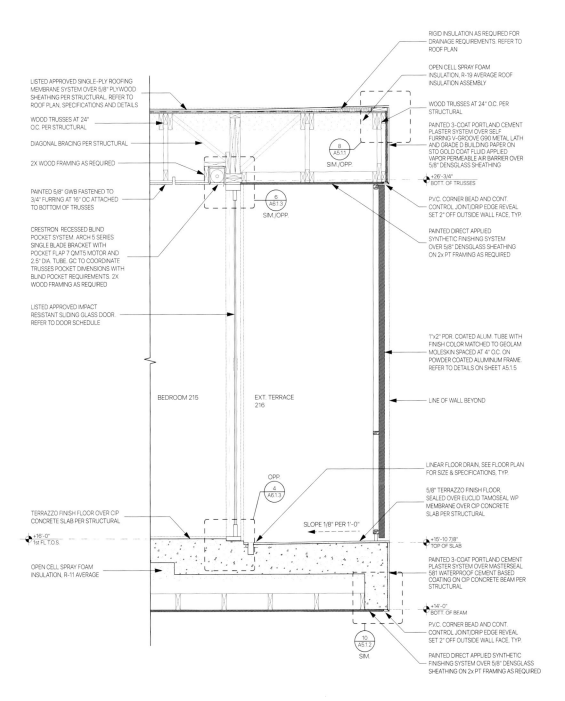

Wall Section

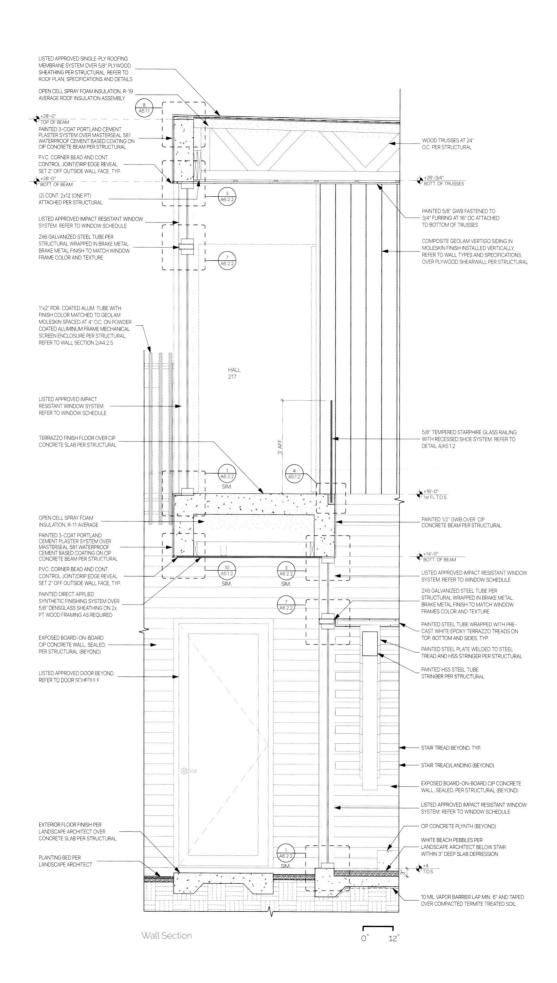

Wall Section

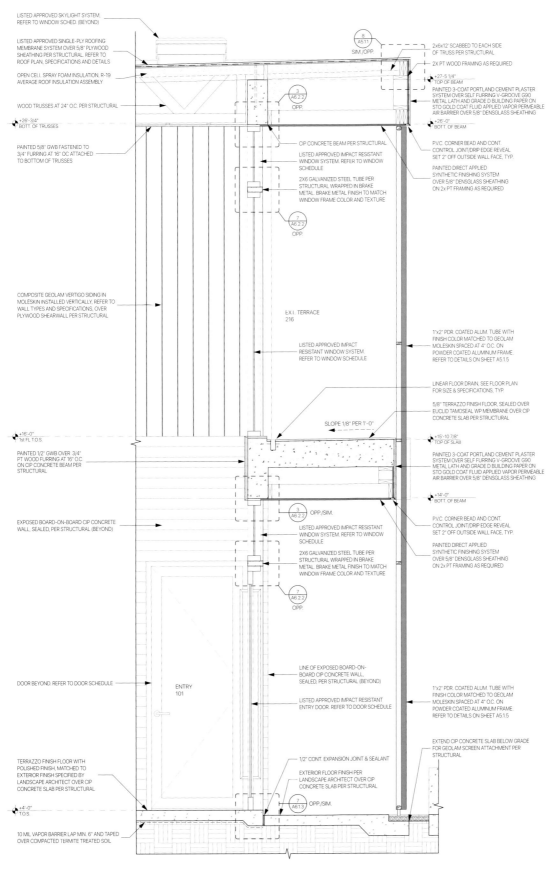

Wall Section

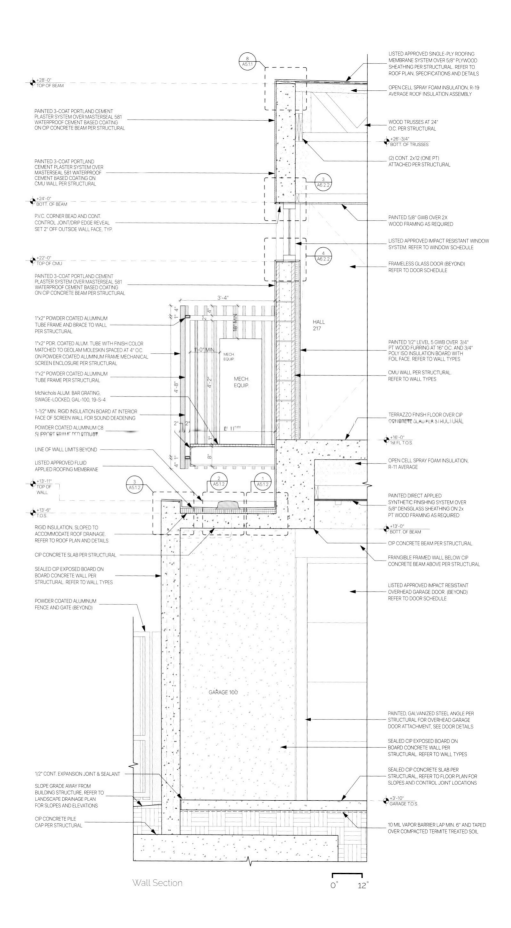

Wall Section

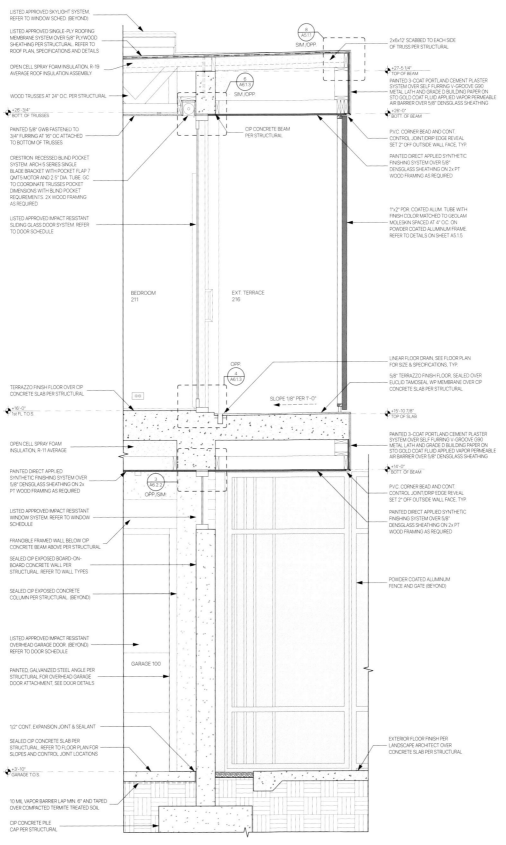

Wall Section

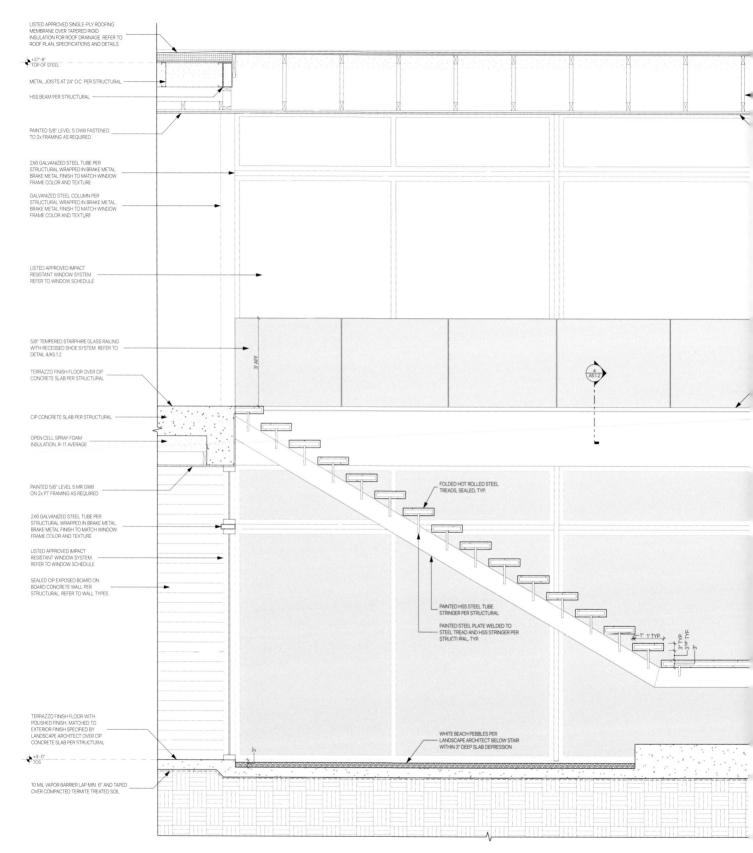

Stair Section

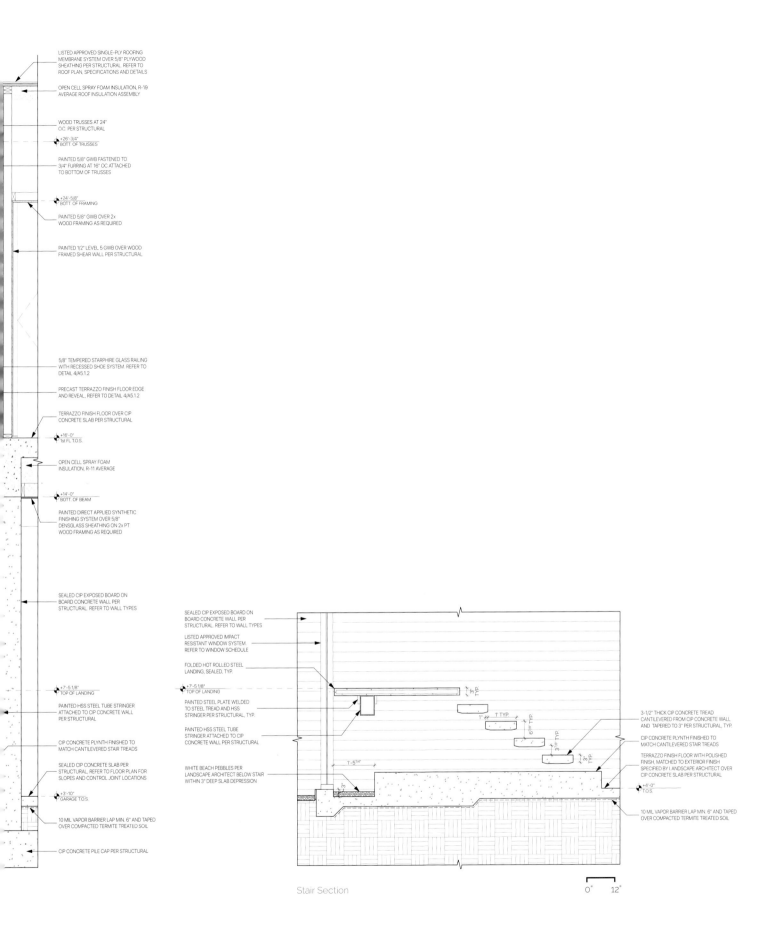

Stair Section

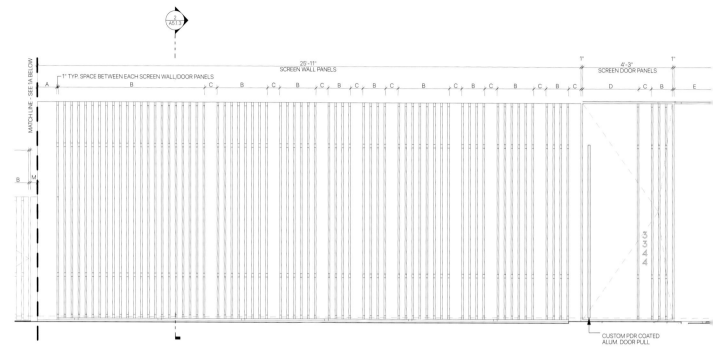

Screen Wall Elevation

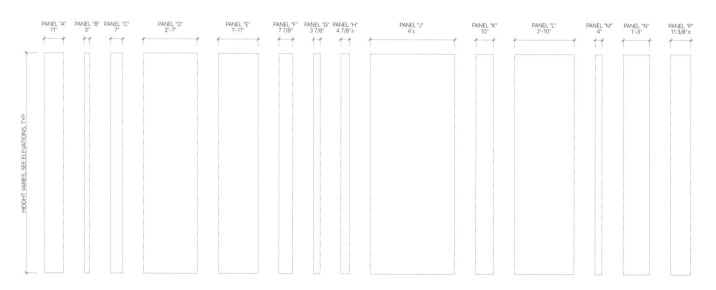

Screen Wall Panel Schedule

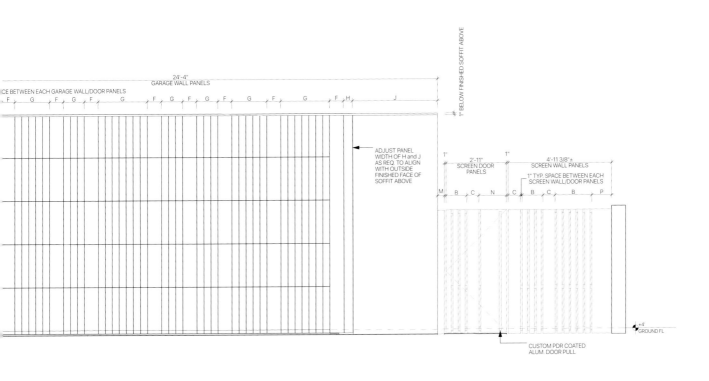
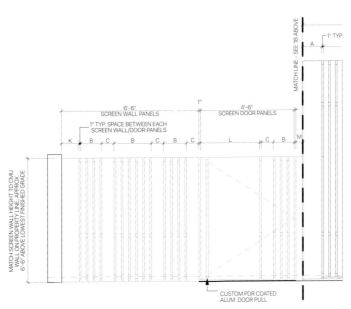

Screen Wall Elevation

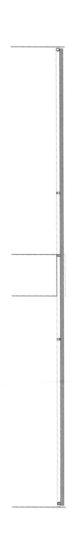
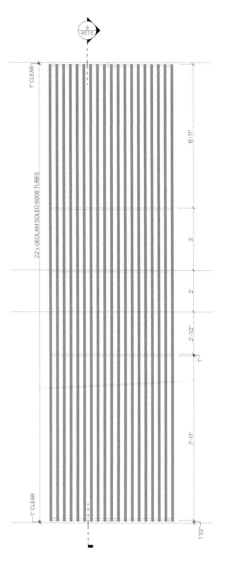

Typ. Sun Screen Long Section

Typ. Sun Screen Long Elevation

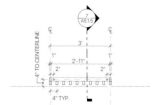

Enlarged Plan - Sun Screen Type "E"

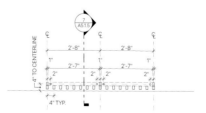

Enlarged Plan - Sun Screen Type "D"

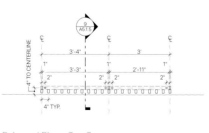

Enlarged Plan - Sun Screen Type "C"

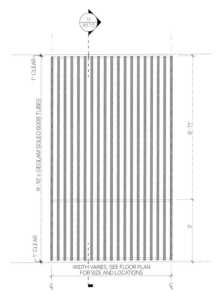

Typ. Wall Mtd. Sun Screen Section

Typ. Wall Mtd. Sun Screen Elevation

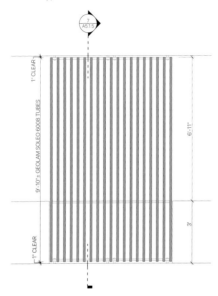

Typ. Sun Screen Section

Typ. Sun Screen Elevation

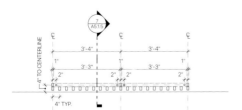

Enlarged Plan - Sun Screen Type "B"

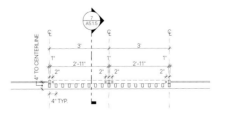

Enlarged Plan - Sun Screen Type "A"

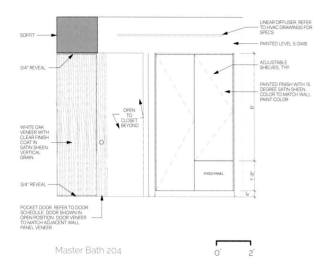

Master Bath 204

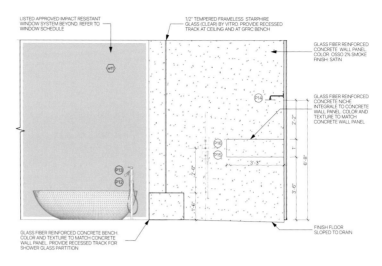

Master Bath 204

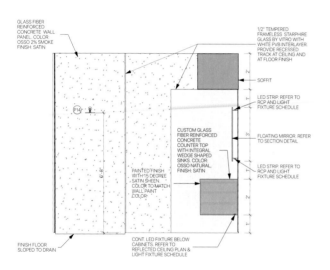

Master Bath 204

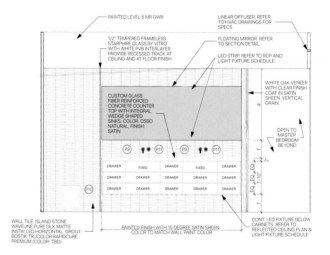

Master Bath 204

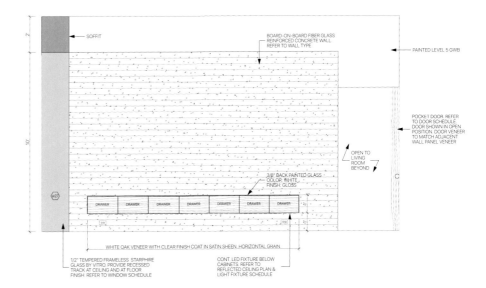

Master Bedroom 203

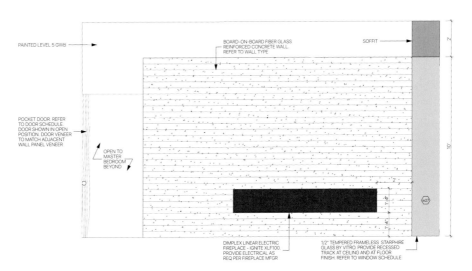

Living Room 202

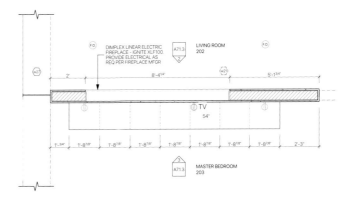

Enlarged Floor Plan

PROCESS

088 | CONSTRUCTION / PROCESS

090 | CONSTRUCTION / PROCESS

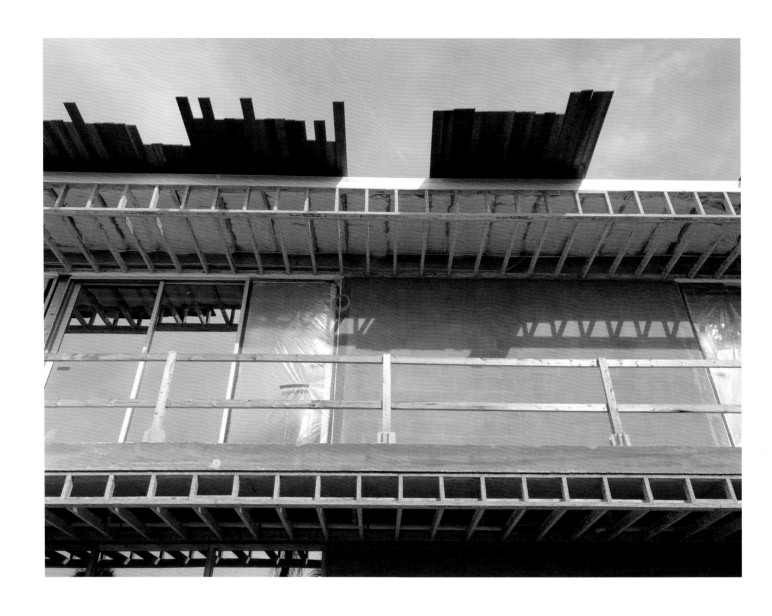

100 | CONSTRUCTION / PROCESS

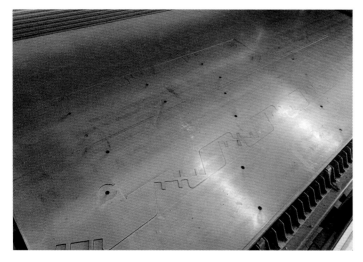
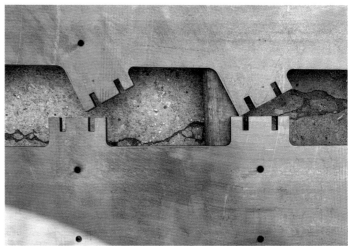

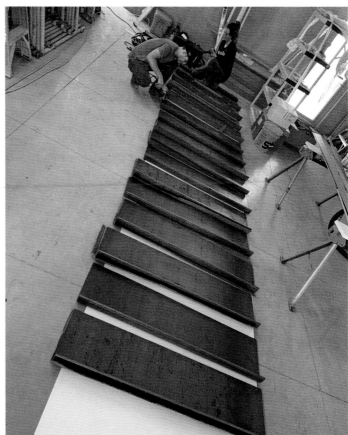

118 | CONSTRUCTION / PROCESS

THE BUILDING

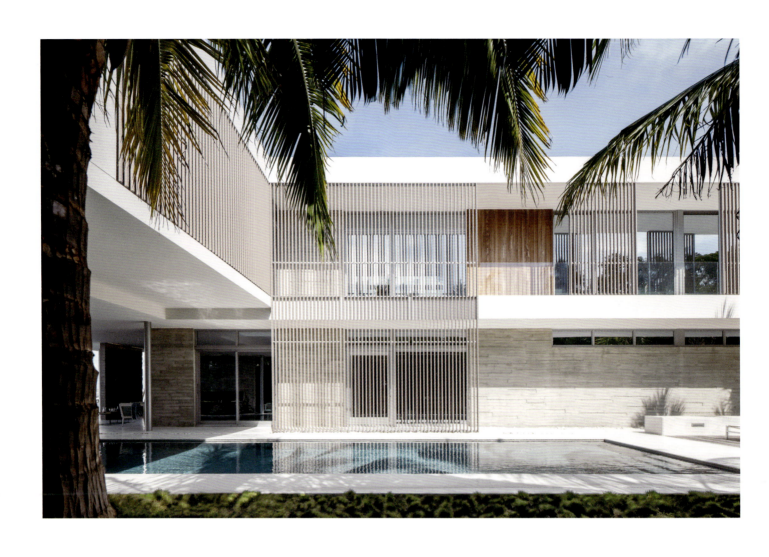

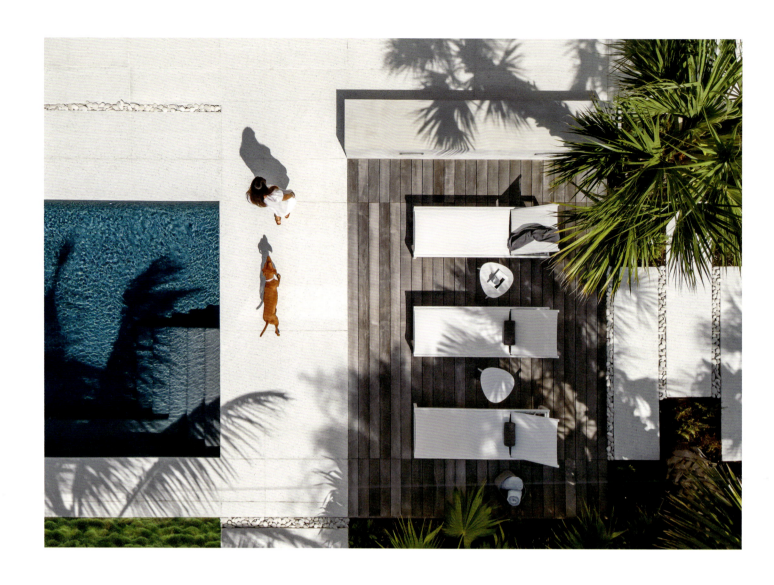

138 | THE BUILDING

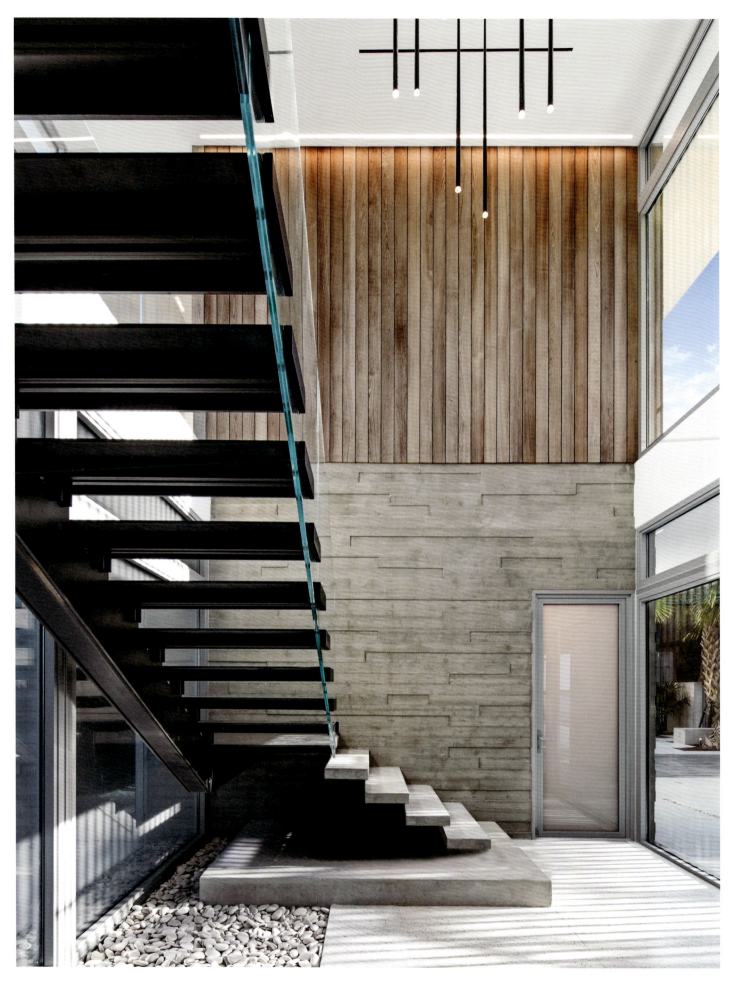

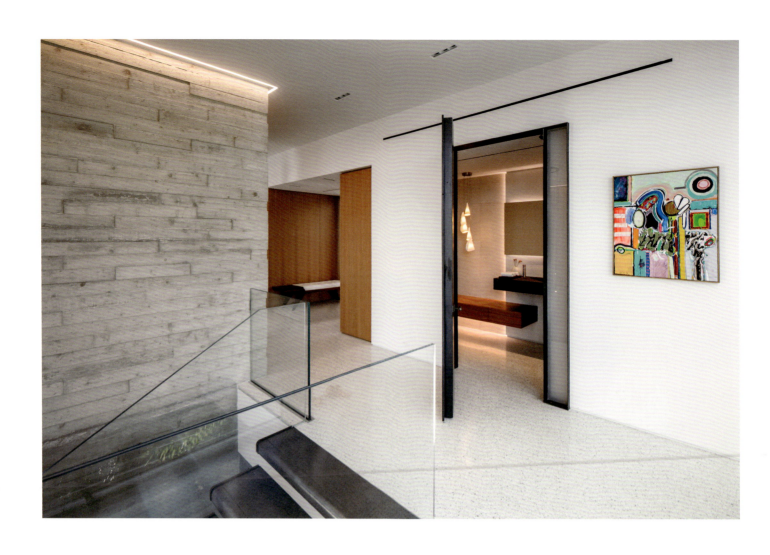

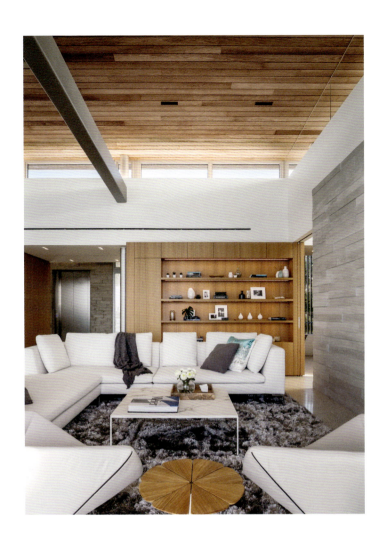

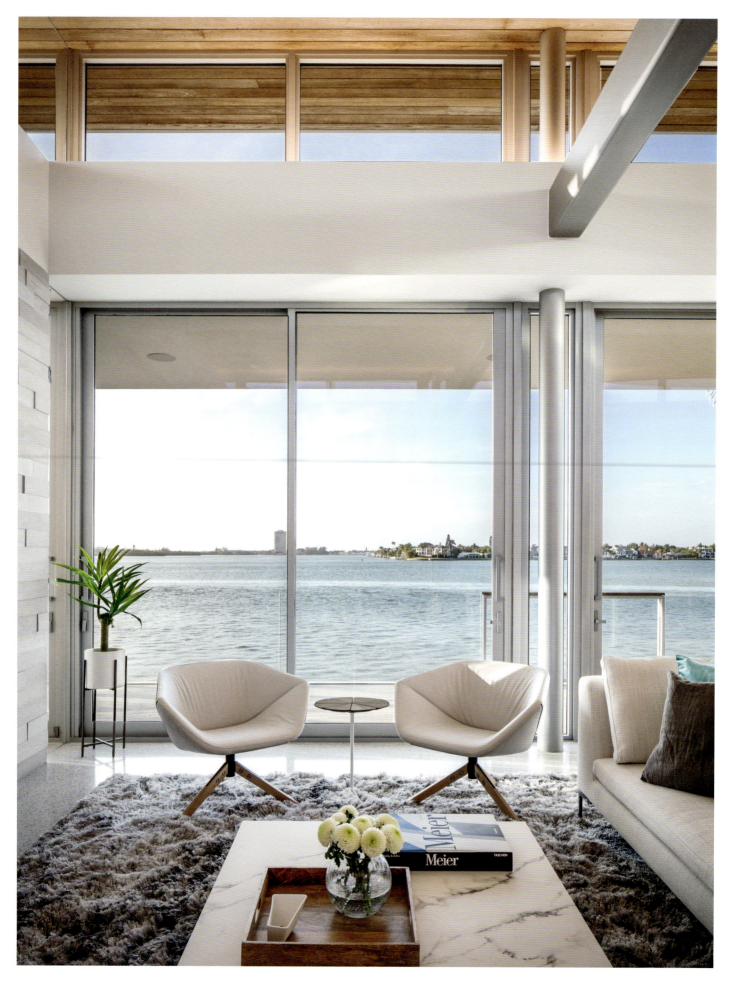

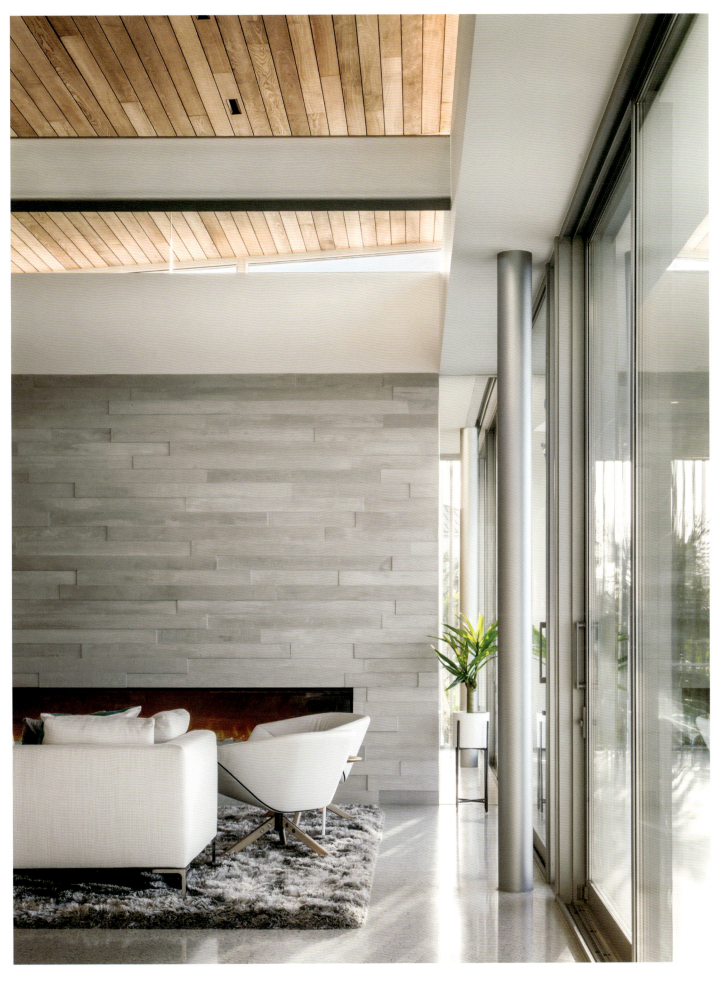

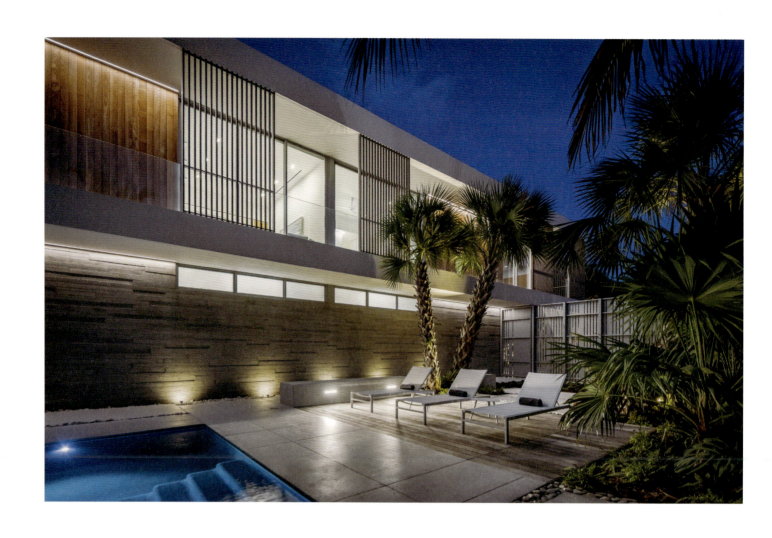

212 | THE BUILDING

APPENDIX

BIOGRAPHY

Hive Architects is an award winning architectural practice based in Sarasota, Florida. Principal architects, Joe Kelly AIA and Gwen Leroy-Kelly AIA, a husband and wife team, share responsibility for developing the vision of the practice. Influenced by architectural concepts engendered by the Sarasota School of Architecture movement, their designs include simple volumes and lines with a strong emphasis on the expression of the structural systems, as well as site specific planning strategies and architectural components that respond to Florida's subtropical climate. Hive Architects is a full service Architectural and Interior Design firm offering professional design services for a diverse range of project types, but is best known for its private houses.

To obtain a deeper meaning in the experience of each project, the work of Hive Architects focuses on concept driven design. The Firm's philosophy and approach to modernism is based on an analysis of the regional and climatic aspects of the site, the client's programmatic and functional desires, and the crafted selection of materials and building systems. Through this investigation and the distillation of all project aspects, Hive endeavors to develop a concept, or organizing idea, that continues to influence and inspire the design process. With no preconceived notions of form, the resulting architecture embodies the character of its local environment, culture, and ultimately the human experience of its inhabitants.

From concept to completion, the work of Hive Architects is based upon a symbiotic interdisciplinary collaboration that includes their clients and consultants. The team's continued interaction and communication of various perspectives results in a refined architectural solution.

Why hive... The name 'Hive' originates from two basic concepts.

First, nature's most efficient and stable building block is the hexagon. From the large scale of the Giant's Causeway basalt column formations on the coast of Ireland, to quartz crystals, to small but always unique snowflakes, or to microscopic molecules, the hexagon is always the main structural building block. The efficiency of the hexagon comes from its ability to interlock with other hexagons where there is no wasted space and space is optimized. That is why bees use the hexagonal honeycomb when developing their own structure: the hive. This concept represents the firm's craft: Architecture.

The second concept is based on the 'Hive Mind' notion that refers to the desire of working together where each individual performs a specific role for the good of the group. The 'Hive Mind' also refers to the collective thoughts, ideas, and opinions of a group of people regarded as functioning together as a single mind. It is about communication, collaboration and coming to a consensus together. Similarly to bees, the collective mental activity is expressed in the complex, coordinated behavior of a colony regarded as comparable to a single mind controlling the behavior of an individual organism. This concept represents the way the firm functions as a team.

Joe Kelly AIA is one of the founding Principals of Hive Architects Inc., a Sarasota-based architecture firm that is consistently recognized for its concept driven and regionally appropriate designs. A Florida native, Joe graduated summa cum lade with a Bachelor of Design in 2001 and Master of Architecture in 2003 from the University of Florida, College of Design, Construction, and Planning. His work focuses on purposeful modernism that heightens the user's perception and connection with space. Through carefully crafted design solutions rooted in regional modernism, Joe's work can be characterized as having a rigorously clear, concise and timeless aesthetic. In 2019, Joe received the Young Architects Design Award from the University of Florida School of Architecture for his significant design contributions in the architectural profession.

Gwen Leroy-Kelly AIA is one of the founding Principals of Hive Architects Inc. A native of France, she graduated summa cum lade with a Bachelor of Design in 2001 and Master of Architecture in 2003 from the University of Florida, College of Design, Construction, and Planning. She specializes in commercial work that exhibits a strong commitment to clarity of thought, design integrity, and quality of architectural detail. With her background and expertise, Hive Architects has become a multi-disciplinary practice that includes interior design, residential architecture, historic preservation, as well as private and public commercial projects. In 2019, Gwen received the Young Architects Design Award from the University of Florida for her significant design contributions in the architectural profession.

PROJECT CREDITS

Architect:
Hive Architects Inc.

Location:
Siesta Key | Sarasota, Florida | USA

Client:
Kate & Richard Nord

Project:
2018

Completion:
2020

Land Area:
21,885 square feet (.5 acre)

Built Area:
4,100 square feet (Interior A/C)

Interior Design:
Hive Architects Inc.

Lighting Design:
Hive Architects Inc.

Design Team:
Joe Kelly, AIA
Gwen Leroy-Kelly, AIA

Photography:
Ryan Gamma
Joe Kelly, AIA

Construction Process Photography:
Joe Kelly, AIA
Gwen Leroy-Kelly, AIA

Landscape Architect:
DWY Landscape Architects
David W. Young, LA - Principal
Krystyna M. Sznurkowski –
Senior Associate

CONSTRUCTION

Mechanical Engineer:
ESC, Karl White

Architectural Concrete:
BMMI, Bob Miller Masonry

Exterior Windows and Doors:
ES Windows

Exterior Plaster:
Commercial Plastering, Billy Rice

**Exterior Screens, Stairs
& Metalwork Details and Fabrication:**
modulo, Giancarlo Giusti

**Cabinetry, Built-ins
& Interior Wall Panels:**
Westwood Manufacturing,
Russ Edwards & Alex Lenza

PHOTOGRAPHY CAPTIONS

Parking court and entry approach.
Photograph by Ryan Gamma.

Entry screen wall with cantilvered guest bedroom suite and exterior terrace.
Photograph by Ryan Gamma.

Parking court and entry approach.
Photograph by Ryan Gamma.

Parking court and entry approach.
Photograph by Ryan Gamma.

Entry screen wall with concealed garage door and cantilvered guest bedroom suite.
Photograph by Ryan Gamma.

Construction process.
Pile cap foundation, rebar installation and formwork.
Photograph by Hive Architects.

Construction process.
Pile cap foundation, rebar installation and formwork.
Photograph by Hive Architects.

Construction process.
Pile cap foundation, rebar installation and formwork.
Photograph by Hive Architects.

Construction process.
Garage foundations.
Photograph by Hive Architects.

Construction process.
Board formed concrete mockup.
Photograph by Hive Architects.

Construction process.
Garage wall concrete forms installed.
Photograph by HiveArchitects.

Construction process.
Ground level concrete garage wall forms being stripped.
Photograph by Hive Architects.

Construction process.
Ground level concrete garage wall forms being stripped.
Photograph by Hive Architects.

Construction process.
Ground level concrete garage wall forms being stripped.
Photograph by Hive Architects.

Construction process.
Ground level concrete garage wall forms being stripped.
Photograph by Hive Architects.

Construction process.
Ground level concrete garage wall forms being stripped.
Photograph by Hive Architects.

Construction process.
Ground level concrete garage wall forms being stripped.
Photograph by Hive Architects.

Construction process.
Scaffolding installation.
Photograph by Hive Architects.

Construction process.
Concrete wall texture detail.
Photograph by Hive Architects.

Construction process.
Scaffolding installation.
Photograph by Hive Architects.

Construction process.
Scaffolding installation.
Photograph by Hive Architects.

Construction process.
First floor concrete slab steel rebar installation and formwork.
Photograph by Hive Architects.

Construction process.
First floor concrete slab steel rebar installation and formwork.
Photograph by Hive Architects.

Construction process.
First floor masonry installation.
Photograph by Hive Architects.

Construction process.
First floor concrete slab steel rebar detail.
Photograph by Hive Architects.

Construction process.
First floor concrete slab steel rebar installation and formwork.
Photograph by Hive Architects.

Construction process.
First floor concrete slab steel rebar detail.
Photograph by Hive Architects.

Construction process.
Garage wall view.
Photograph by Hive Architects.

Construction process.
Scaffolding installation for first floor concrete slab.
Photograph by Hive Architects.

Construction process.
Locating approximate location of linear kitchen window with framed views of downtown Sarasota.
Photograph by Hive Architects.

Construction process.
First floor masonry installation.
Photograph by Hive Architects.

Construction process.
First floor masonry installation.
Photograph by Hive Architects.

Construction process.
Ground floor entry space.
Photograph by Hive Architects.

Construction process.
Ground floor entry space.
Photograph by Hive Architects.

Construction process.
Completed masonry installation.
Photograph by Hive Architects.

Construction process.
Ground floor view up to
east facing entry wall.
Photograph by Hive Architects.

Construction process.
Kitchen window openings
with framed views.
Photograph by Hive Architects.

Construction process.
View of dining and kitchen space
with roof framing in process.
Photograph by Hive Architects.

Construction process.
Structural steel and roof framing.
Photograph by Hive Architects.

Construction process.
Roof framing.
Photograph by Hive Architects.

Construction process.
Ground floor entry space.
Photograph by Hive Architects.

Construction process.
Double height entry space with
window installation in process.
Photograph by Hive Architects.

Construction process.
Garage space with windows
ready for installation.
Photograph by Hive Architects.

Construction process.
Guest wing sliding
door installation.
Photograph by Hive Architects.

Construction process.
Elevated exterior terrace slab
preparation for terrazzo installation.
Photograph by Hive Architects.

Construction process.
Exterior terrace sliding
door installation.
Photograph by Hive Architects.

Construction process.
View from elevated enry
space before window
and screen installation.
Photograph by Hive Architects.

Construction process.
Guest wing soffit
framing installation.
Photograph by Hive Architects.

Construction process.
Soffit framing installation.
Photograph by Hive Architects.

Construction process.
Mechanical ductwork installation.
Photograph by Hive Architects.

Construction process.
Guest wing soffit framing.
Photograph by Hive Architects.

Construction process.
Interior floor preparation
for terrazzo installation.
Photograph by Hive Architects.

Construction process.
Guest wing soffit framing and
insulation with thermo-ash wood
siding pre-weathering on roof.
Photograph by Hive Architects.

Construction process.
Roofing installation.
Photograph by Hive Architects.

Construction process.
Clerestory glass.
Photograph by Hive Architects.

Construction process.
Guest wing soffit framing and
insulation installation with
thermo-ash wood siding
pre-weathering on roof.
Photograph by Hive Architects.

Construction process.
Exterior wall plastering.
Photograph by Hive Architects.

Construction process.
Exterior plastering.
Photograph by Hive Architects.

Construction process.
Exterior soffit plastering.
Photograph by Hive Architects.

Construction process.
Exterior soffit plastering.
Photography by Hive Architects.

Construction process.
Interior framing.
Photograph by Hive Architects.

Construction process.
Drywall installation.
Photograph by Hive Architects.

Construction process.
Electrical wiring.
Photograph by Hive Architects.

Construction process.
Drywall installation.
Photograph by Hive Architects.

Construction process.
Ceiling preparation for
pre-weathered thermo-ash
wood installation.
Photograph by Hive Architects.

Construction process.
Plastering completed with
thermo-ash wood siding
pre-weathering on roof.
Photograph by Hive Architects.

Construction process.
Plastering completed with
temporary access stair in place.
Photograph by Hive Architects.

Construction process.
Pool enclosure
structure foundation.
Photograph by Hive Architects.

Construction process.
Entry courtyard with
pool shell completed.
Photograph by Hive Architects.

Construction process.
Pool shell view.
Photograph by Hive Architects.

Construction process.
Pool shell with view to
concrete wall fire feature.
Photograph by Hive Architects.

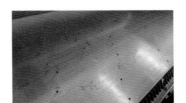

Construction process.
Hot rolled steel entry
stair fabrication.
Photograph by Giancarlo Giusti.

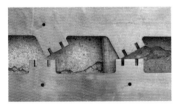

Construction process.
Hot rolled steel entry
stair fabrication.
Photograph by Giancarlo Giusti.

Construction process.
Hot rolled steel entry
stair fabrication.
Photograph by Giancarlo Giusti.

Construction process.
Hot rolled steel entry
stair fabrication.
Photograph by Giancarlo Giusti.

Construction process.
Hot rolled steel entry
stair fabrication.
Photograph by Giancarlo Giusti.

Construction process.
Hot rolled steel entry
stair fabrication.
Photograph by Giancarlo Giusti.

Construction process.
Hot rolled steel entry
stair installation.
Photograph by Hive Architects.

Construction process.
Concrete entry stair installation.
Photograph by Hive Architects.

Construction process.
Hot rolled steel entry
stair installation.
Photograph by Hive Architects.

Construction process.
Hot rolled steel entry stair.
Photograph by Hive Architects.

Construction process.
Hot rolled steel entry stair.
Photograph by Hive Architects.

Construction process.
Hot rolled steel entry stair.
Photograph by Hive Architects.

Construction process.
Hot rolled steel entry stair.
Photograph by Hive Architects.

Construction process.
Hot rolled steel entry stair.
Photograph by Hive Architects.

Construction process.
Entry stair installation.
Photograph by Hive Architects.

Construction process.
Entry stair treads detail.
Photograph by Hive Architects.

Construction process.
Entry stair glass railing templates.
Photograph by Hive Architects.

Construction process.
Entry pendant light installation.
Photograph by Hive Architects.

Construction process.
Terrazzo installation at north
facing exterior terrace.
Photograph by Hive Architects.

Construction process.
Terrazzo installation.
Photograph by Hive Architects.

Construction process.
Terrazzo installation.
Photograph by Hive Architects.

Construction process.
Landscape installation
Photograph by Hive Architects.

Construction process.
Landscape installation.
Photograph by Hive Architects.

Construction process.
Thermo-ash wood
siding installation.
Photograph by Hive Architects.

Construction process.
Thermo-ash wood siding
and glass railing installation.
Photograph by Hive Architects.

Construction process.
Custom bed joint detail.
Photograph by Giancarlo Giusti.

Construction process.
Custom bed in fabrication.
Photograph by Giancarlo Giusti.

Construction process.
Custom bed structure.
Photograph by Giancarlo Giusti.

Construction process.
Custom bed installed onsite.
Photograph by Giancarlo Giusti.

Construction process.
Custom glass pocket door hangers.
Photograph by Giancarlo Giusti.

Construction process.
Custom glass pocket
door hanger detail.
Photograph by Giancarlo Giusti.

Construction process.
Custom sun screen fabrication.
Photograph by Giancarlo Giusti.

Construction process.
Custom sun screen fabrication.
Photograph by Giancarlo Giusti.

Construction process.
Custom sun screen
installation at entry garden.
Photograph by Giancarlo Giusti.

Construction process.
Custom entry screen
wall installation.
Photograph by Giancarlo Giusti.

Construction process.
Custom entry screen
wall installation.
Photograph by Giancarlo Giusti.

Construction process.
Parking court pavers.
Photograph by Giancarlo Giusti.

Construction process.
Entry stair sun and shadow pattern.
Photograph by Hive Architects.

Construction process.
Entry stair sun and shadow pattern.
Photograph by Hive Architects.

Construction process.
Guest bedroom sun
and shadow pattern.
Photograph by Hive Architects.

Construction process.
Dining room pendant
light and cabinetry installed.
Photograph by Hive Architects.

Construction process.
Master bedroom cabinetry.
Photograph by Hive Architects.

Construction process.
TV room sliding door.
Photograph by Hive Architects.

Construction process.
Dining and living room cabinets with finished drywall and wood ceiling.
Photograph by Hive Architects.

Construction process.
Kitchen cabinets.
Photograph by Hive Architects.

Construction process.
Front (south facing) elevation with installed entry court pavers and screen wall.
Photograph by Hive Architects.

Parking court.
Photograph by Ryan Gamma.

Entry screen wall with cantilvered guest bedroom suite and exterior terrace.
Photograph by Ryan Gamma.

Entry screen wall with concealed garage door and cantilvered guest bedroom suite.
Photograph by Ryan Gamma.

Elevated view of the front entry with private garden beyond.
Photograph by Ryan Gamma.

Entry Courtyard.
Photograph by Joe Kelly.

Pool sun deck.
Photograph by Ryan Gamma.

Detail view of pool sun deck.
Photograph by Ryan Gamma.

Pool sun deck with view towards Sarasota Bay.
Photograph by Ryan Gamma.

Double height entry and screen wall.
Photograph by Ryan Gamma.

Lap pool with view to entry screen wall and Sarasota Bay beyond.
Photograph by Ryan Gamma.

Double height entry and screen wall.
Photograph by Joe Kelly.

 Aerial view of pool and sun deck. Photograph by Ryan Gamma.

 Pool and sun deck with entry screen wall beyond. Photograph by Ryan Gamma.

 Covered outdoor living space adjacent to pool with downtown views beyond. Photograph by Ryan Gamma.

 Covered pool with view to fire feature within concrete shear wall. Photograph by Ryan Gamma.

 The mesic 'zen' hammock garden creates a backdrop to the entry stair hall. Photograph by Ryan Gamma.

 Hot rolled steel entry stair with zen garden at exterior. Photograph by Ryan Gamma.

 Hot rolled steel entry stair with zen garden at exterior. Photograph by Ryan Gamma.

 Upon arrival, guests are greeted by a double height entry space with views to the oudoor mesic 'zen' hammock garden that creates a backdrop to the cantilvered stair. Photograph byRyan Gamma.

 Entry stair detail with cantilevered concrete treads. Photograph by Ryan Gamma.

 Double height entry space, view from upper level to offset pivot entry door. Photograph by Ryan Gamma.

 Double height entry space with refined material palette that encompasses the conceptual aspect of Shibusa. Photograph by Joe Kelly.

 The double height entry core also serves as a transition from public to private spaces and bridges between the main living spaces and guest wing. Photograph by Ryan Gamma.

 Powder bath, concealed by a custom hot rolled steel door and translucent glass sidelite. Photograph by Ryan Gamma.

 Powder bath, magnetic latch hardware detail. Photograph by Ryan Gamma.

 Living room with view to dining room and kitchen. The interior spaces establish a constant connection to the exterior long views of Big Sarasota Pass and to the downtown Sarasota skyline. Photograph by Ryan Gamma.

 Living room with glass fiber reinforced concrete wall and linear fireplace. Spaces flow seamlessly from one to another while providing an enriched, subdued appearance and experience of instrinsically fine quality with econmy of form, line and effort. Photograph by Ryan Gamma.

Living room custom cabinetry.
Photograph by Ryan Gamma.

Living room.
Photograph by Ryan Gamma.

The living and dining rooms are defined by a hovering wood clad roof form with long views to Big Sarasota Pass and the surrounding islands. Photograph by Ryan Gamma.

Dining room and kitchen with concealed hardware.
Photograph by Ryan Gamma.

Dining room.
Photograph by Ryan Gamma.

Dining room and kitchen with concealed hardware.
Photograph by Ryan Gamma.

Dining room and kitchen with concealed hardware.
Photograph by Ryan Gamma.

Kitchen.
Photograph by Ryan Gamma.

Kitchen.
Photograph by Ryan Gamma.

View from kitchen to living room.
Photograph by Ryan Gamma.

Living room.
Photograph by Ryan Gamma.

View from kitchen to living room.
Photograph by Ryan Gamma.

Master bedroom, view to south.
Photograph by Ryan Gamma.

Master bedroom, view to north.
Photograph by Ryan Gamma.

Master bedroom.
Photograph by Ryan Gamma.

Master bedroom cabinetry and glass fiber reinforced concrete wall detail.
Photograph by Ryan Gamma.

 Master bedroom view from living room. Photograph by Ryan Gamma.

 Master bathroom, detail. Photograph by Ryan Gamma.

 Master bathroom, detail. Photograph by Ryan Gamma.

 Master bathroom, view west. Photograph by Ryan Gamma.

 Master bathroom, view east. Photograph by Ryan Gamma.

 Master bathroom, glass pocket door and hardware detail. Photograph by Ryan Gamma.

 Laundry room. Photograph by Ryan Gamma.

 The double height entry core also serves as transition from public to private spaces and bridges between the main living spaces and guest wing. Photograph by Ryan Gamma.

 TV room, view west. Photograph by Ryan Gamma.

 TV room, view east with sliding wall closed. Photograph by Ryan Gamma.

 TV room, view east with sliding wall. Photograph by Ryan Gamma.

 TV room, view east with sliding wall. Photograph by Ryan Gamma.

 TV room, view east with sliding wall open. Photograph by Ryan Gamma.

 TV room, sliding wall and terrazzo floor finish detail. Photograph by Ryan Gamma.

 TV room built-ins. Photograph by Ryan Gamma.

 Guest hall, view north to main entry space. Photograph by Ryan Gamma.

TV room, view north.
Photograph by Ryan Gamma.

Guest wing exterior terrace, view south.
Photograph by Ryan Gamma.

Guest bedroom suite, view west.
Photograph by Ryan Gamma.

Guest bedroom suite, view west.
Photograph by Ryan Gamma.

Guest bedroom suite.
Photograph by Ryan Gamma.

Guest bathroom.
Photograph by Ryan Gamma.

Guest bedroom suite, view north.
Photograph by Ryan Gamma.

Guest wing exterior terrace, view north.
Photograph by Ryan Gamma.

Guest bathroom.
Photograph by Ryan Gamma.

Guest bedroom suite, view north.
Photograph by Ryan Gamma.

Guest bedroom suite, view south
Photograph by Ryan Gamma.

Guest wing exterior terrace, view north toward living room entry door.
Photograph by Ryan Gamma.

Living and dining rooms.
Photograph by Ryan Gamma.

North facing elevation at sunset.
Photograph by Ryan Gamma.

North facing elevation at sunset.
Photograph by Ryan Gamma.

Night view of pool and sun deck.
Photograph by Ryan Gamma.

Night view of pool and sun deck with guest wind above. Photograph by Ryan Gamma.

Night view of pool and sun deck. Photograph by Ryan Gamma.

Night view of pool and sun deck. Photograph by Ryan Gamma.

Night view of pool and entry. Photograph by Ryan Gamma.

Night view of pool and outdoor living. Photograph by Ryan Gamma.

Night view of pool, entry and sun deck. Photograph by Ryan Gamma.

Night view of pool and outdoor living. Photograph by Ryan Gamma.

Night view of pool and outdoor living with long views of downtown Sarasota. Photograph by Ryan Gamma.

Night view of parking court and front elevation. Photograph by Ryan Gamma.

Night view of entry screen wall with cantilvered guest bedroom suite and exterior terrace. Photograph by Ryan Gamma.

Night view of screen wall with concealed garage door and cantilvered guest bedroom suite. Photograph by Ryan Gamma.

Night view of parking court and entry approach. Photograph by Ryan Gamma.

Night view of screen wall with concealed garage door and cantilvered guest bedroom suite. Photograph by Ryan Gamma.

BOOK CREDITS

Graphic design by Lucía Bauzá
Art direction by Oscar Riera Ojeda
Copy Editing by Kit Maude & Michael W. Phillips Jr.
Introduction by Robert McCarter/Copyright © 2021 Robert McCarter

OSCAR RIERA OJEDA
PUBLISHERS

Copyright © 2022 Hive Architects Inc. & Oscar Riera Ojeda Publishers Limited
ISBN 978-1-946226-54-9
Published by Oscar Riera Ojeda Publishers Limited
Printed in China

Oscar Riera Ojeda Publishers Limited
Unit 1003-04, 10/F.,
Shanghai Industrial Investment Building,
48-62 Hennessy Road, Wanchai, Hong Kong

Production Offices | China
Suit 19, Shenyun Road,
Nanshan District, Shenzhen 518055

International Customer Service & Editorial Questions: +1-484-502-5400

www.oropublishers.com | www.oscarrieraojeda.com
oscar@oscarrieraojeda.com

All rights reserved. No part of this book may be reproduced, stored in a retrieval system, or transmitted in any form or by any means, including electronic, mechanical, photocopying of microfilming, recording, or otherwise (except that copying permitted by Sections 107 and 108 of the U.S. Copyright Law and except by reviewers for the public press) without written permission from the publisher.